Anti-Anxious:
How to Control Your Thoughts, Stop Overthinking, and Transform Your Mental Habits

by Nick Trenton

www.NickTrenton.com

Table of Contents

CHAPTER 1: REFRAME YOUR INTERNAL DIALOGUE AND TAKE CONTROL OF YOUR SELF-TALK — 7

- PROBLEM 1: THE ALL-OR-NOTHING DISEASE — 13
- PROBLEM 2: "OUT OF POWER" LANGUAGE — 18
- WHAT TO DO ABOUT IT — 22
- HOW TO IDENTIFY YOUR COGNITIVE DISTORTIONS — 27

CHAPTER 2: ANALYZE THYSELF: THE ABC METHOD AND THOUGHT JOURNALS — 47

- STEP 1: HOW TO KEEP A THOUGHT JOURNAL — 55
- STEP 2: RETHINK . . . AND REDO — 58
- DECENTER, SHIFT PERSPECTIVE, AND CREATE DISTANCE — 65
- HOW TO TAKE A STEP BACK — 68
- A WORD ON THE MOST USELESS HABIT IN THE WORLD — 75
- TRY A COGNITIVE DEFUSION EXERCISE — 80

CHAPTER 3: MASTER THE ART OF DISTRESS TOLERANCE AND SELF-SOOTHING — 99

- HOW TO SELF-SOOTHE — 103
- TIPP SKILLS — 107
- WHAT RADICAL ACCEPTANCE REALLY MEANS — 113
- THE ACCEPTS SKILL — 117

Brain Dumping, Mental Noting, and Scheduled Worry Time — 120

CHAPTER 4: UPGRADE YOUR PSYCHOLOGICAL TOOLKIT WITH STOIC *AMOR FATI* PHILOSOPHY — 135

Beyond Radical Acceptance: Amor Fati — 136
Negative Visualization — 143
What is Your Orientation: Solution or Problem Orientation? Thought or Action? — 155

CHAPTER 5: AVOID THE TRAP OF TOXIC POSITIVITY AND FEEL YOUR FEELINGS — 169

The Positive IS Powerful, But . . . — 172
Good Versus Whole — 176
Letting Go of Toxic Positivity — 178
One Underappreciated Way to Genuinely Feel Better — 184
Emotional Regulation — 185
The Life Cycle of an Emotion — 190

CHAPTER 6: BUT WHERE DOES NEGATIVE THINKING REALLY COME FROM? — 203

Your Negativity May Be "Hardwired" — 206
Countering the Bias for the Negative — 212

Rethink Toxic Relationships—Including the One You Have with Yourself   **215**

SUMMARY GUIDE   231

Chapter 1: Reframe Your Internal Dialogue and Take Control of Your Self-Talk

If you've picked up this book, there's a good chance that you've noticed that your own internal thought processes are . . . not what they could be. Pervasive negative thinking is the kind of problem that initially seems to fly under the radar. A person with a predisposition to interpret everything in a negative light can convince themselves for a long time that they are completely neutral and objective observers, and the negativity simply lies in what they're observing. That there seems to be an awful lot of negativity "out there" only dimly arouses their suspicion!

Pervasive negative thinking is like having a poisoned pot in your kitchen, so that everything you cook in that pot becomes poisoned, too. You think you have one problem: *Everything* you eat seems to make you sick! But in fact, you have another, perhaps more serious problem—you continue to use the poisoned pot.

If you regularly find yourself saying things like, "Everything is awful," then you can be pretty sure that you have a poisoned pot in your mental kitchen. So much personal development and self-help material out there is designed to help you fix the problems that your mind has told you are there:

How do I stop being so lazy and unmotivated?

How do I get over being so fat and out of shape?

How do I stop being such a loser?

But you can see the problem. The solution you really need is to be curious about the mindset that allows you to think that you are a fat, lazy loser in the first place!

You already know that the way you think influences how you see yourself, the world, and everyone around you. But it goes even further than this. **How you think doesn't just influence your life, it *is* your life.** If the mind is the means by which we tell our story, interpret those stories, and ascribe meaning to our experiences, then the mind is more or less in charge of all of it.

The way we think determines what we believe is possible, how we solve problems, what we can expect in the future, and how to plan for it, and therefore how we act.

The way we think tells us why our experiences happened and what they mean, and therefore our value in that story, i.e., our self-worth.

The way we think highlights certain events as all-important and allows us to forget others so that we reinforce not what is most real, but what most fits our assumptions.

The way we think even decides what enters our conscious awareness in the first place and determines which parts of the big, wide world we never even realize are right there . . .

So, if your thinking is heavily skewed to the negative, you have a serious problem. Humankind has long recognized the possibility of having so warped and distorted a mental filter that the person is assumed to have lost touch with reality entirely. We know that people in severe depressive episodes or those with psychosis or paranoia have not just made a misinterpretation of reality—they cannot see it at all. And yet, how many "normal" people are walking around with a head full of thoughts that are just as unconnected to reality?

If a paranoid schizophrenic says, "I'm queen of the moon and I need to find my way back there before the mole people catch me," we can easily recognize the claim for what it is—nonsense. But if a friend tells you, "I can't come with you to the speed dating thing tonight; that kind of thing just doesn't work for me. Plus, I'm too old," then you might not only take their word for it, you may even start to behave as though it's one hundred percent true! But if you look closely, this second claim has no more evidence to support it than the first. What's more, the second claim can wreak havoc just as surely as the first one can—perhaps, it can cause even more damage.

As you embark on the approaches and techniques covered in the rest of this book, you'll be trying to do something you may not have done before: **think about how you think. This is called metacognition**. Trying to change negative thinking is a peculiar task because we are attempting to change our minds... using our minds. If we bring negativity to the process, we only amplify the problem of negative self-talk rather than address it at its root. Therefore, as you read, try to bear a few things in mind:

- **You will need to think in ways you haven't thought before**. This means that the exercises will *necessarily* feel unfamiliar, awkward, uncomfortable, or even wrong. This isn't a problem or a sign that you should stop. It's only proof that you're stepping outside of your comfort zone. Always remember why they call it a comfort zone—it's comfortable. But that's about all it is! You probably agree with the advice that says, "Don't believe everything you read." In the same way, try not to "believe everything you think."
- **You are not broken or unique in your tendency to think negatively**. In fact, the preference for focusing on the negative has been hardwired into your brain over thousands of years of evolution (more on this in our final chapter). So, you don't need to feel ashamed, and you certainly don't need to feel negative about how negative you feel! Rather than dwelling on the "root cause" or beating yourself up for not being better sooner, just get on with the business of living the life you actually do want to lead.
- **From this moment on, you will no longer take your own word for it**. In other words, you will make a deal with

yourself that from now on, you will understand thoughts for what they are: *thoughts*. Not reality, not truth, not fate or destiny. Just thoughts. Just electrochemical activity in your brain. Be careful, though. This doesn't mean you should become a total skeptic. Don't accept everything that pops into your brain, but at the same time don't dismiss it either—rather, withhold judgment entirely. Be neutral. First, don't react.

- **Finally, at no point in the chapters that follow are you required to be relentlessly "optimistic."** Changing the way you think is not about self-deception, denial, or believing comfortable lies. To say it another way, being a negative thinker is not the same as being more intelligent, more realistic, or more pragmatic. And really, it's about the *quality* of your thinking processes, not the *content*. Some of those relentlessly "positive" people out there have more cognitive distortions than anyone else!

We will explore each of the ideas above in more detail as we go along, but for now, it's enough to simply be aware of one thing: Our ability to genuinely change our thought patterns is not some superhuman ability reserved for just a few people. It rests on two things:

1. **honest awareness, and**
2. **a willingness to take conscious and inspired action.**

That's all. Just those two things. That means that no matter how negative your thought patterns currently are, and no matter how trapped and frustrated you currently feel, it IS possible to change. In fact, by beginning this book, you have already made the first small step in the right direction. Well done!

Problem 1: The All-or-Nothing Disease
Your brain is great at what it does. Its job is to make the world navigable for you—it creates shortcuts, rules ("heuristics"), and predictions so that you can make sense of the events unfolding around you. Your ancestors survived precisely because they were able to do this and, putting it bluntly, make sweeping generalizations and apply stereotypes. And you do it too.

Let's say one day you try Nepalese cuisine and find it absolutely disgusting. You make a conclusion: "I don't like Nepalese food." This conclusion prevents you from repeating the unpleasant experience, and, at least from a neurological perspective, you can be said to have *learned* and expanded your experience of the world. However, there's one inconvenient problem: Your conclusion isn't *true*.

Our mental shortcuts, assumptions, biases and stereotypes are great at saving time and effort but are not one hundred percent accurate one hundred percent of the time. When we take a single experience and extrapolate our conclusions to apply to other experiences we haven't actually had yet, we gain a sense of control and mastery over the situation ... but at the risk of losing accuracy and nuance. Our world becomes more manageable, but that's because it becomes smaller. So, the truth may be that you only dislike around sixty percent of the most common Nepalese dishes, but you've rounded this up to "all Nepalese food" and carried on with life, none the wiser that you've oversimplified reality in this way.

Whenever you use the following words, **oversimplifying reality** is exactly what you're doing:

Never

Always

All

None

Forever

Never

To counter all-too-common black-or-white thinking, people are told to drop these words from their vocabulary. This is a good start, but **it's not the words you need to be on guard for, but the sentiment behind them**. *Any time we overextrapolate from one experience to other experiences we haven't had*, we are making an error.

Thinking in extremes is a problem because it's inaccurate, yes, but <u>the bigger problem is that you are living as though it is true</u>. And this goes far beyond what words you use or don't use.

For example, Jenna finds socializing difficult and is having trouble making friends in a new city. After a few weeks of trying unsuccessfully to join Meetup groups or connect with people at her gym or church, she says the following to a friend back in her hometown: "You know how it is. It's harder to make friends in your thirties, especially if you don't have kids. People just don't have time to socialize. Everyone stays in their own little clique and it's impossible to get to know them." Jenna's friend agrees instantly. Wouldn't you?

The trouble is, although Jenna hasn't used the words "never," "all," or "always," she is still extrapolating to an enormous degree:

Step 1: My current experience is XYZ.

Step 2: Therefore, XYZ is the way it is for *all* people, in *all* times, and will forever be.

Jenna could have said, "I'm having a little difficulty these first few weeks trying to meet people," or "I haven't really connected with anyone at the gym yet." Instead, she concocts a broad theory about all people everywhere. In fact, she makes a pronouncement so grand and all-encompassing that it seems to speak to the human condition as a whole. *People just don't make friends in their thirties.* Can you see how she makes this statement as though it were as naturally obvious and true as the law of gravity?

It **isn't** a natural law. But what Jenna has done is created a world in which it is. Then she lives in that world. She behaves as though it were true. Without even knowing it, she begins to lessen the effort she makes to meet people. She goes through all the motions, but at the back of her mind is this little theory of human nature that she has created, which says, "People aren't *really* interested; you cannot join their little clique, as hard as you try." So, she tries, but not really, and it doesn't go anywhere. People don't respond to her lukewarm efforts, and this reflects her own ambivalence.

Et voila—Jenna finds herself living in a world that looks suspiciously like how she said it would look. This is the natural result of thinking in extremes, using all-or-nothing language, and making grand theories off the back of one or two personal experiences: a self-fulfilling prophecy. When we talk about the world as though it's either black or white, all or nothing, perfect or abysmal . . . then that is precisely the way it becomes.

One final point you might not have considered: other people are usually more than happy to go along with whatever conclusions you've made about life or yourself, and *help you make that true*. Imagine that a friend of Jenna's has been listening to her complain about how difficult it is to meet people in your thirties. One day, Jenna's friend finds an interesting article in the paper about how isolated childfree women can feel. The friend actually doesn't agree with the article, nor care, but she thinks, "You know who will like this? Jenna." She shares the article with Jenna, who reads it and becomes even further entrenched in her narrative, which is quickly cementing itself in her mind.

Can you see what's happened? Jenna's friend, trying to be helpful, is rushing in to confirm and reiterate the (faulty) belief she knows Jenna already has. It is as though Jenna is slowly creating a "filter bubble" around herself, and reality's "search algorithms" keep supplying her with the kind of content she keeps seeking out! Consider that people in your world are doing this too, consciously or unconsciously, all the time. This is the power of a thought pattern—it can be so effective at creating reality that it can even extend to other people. Your environment cannot help but respond to your thought processes—what beliefs is it amplifying?

Problem 2: "Out of Power" Language

Let's stay with Jenna's example, in particular her claim that, "Everyone stays in their own little clique and it's impossible to get to know them." You have probably heard people say things like this before—or maybe you say them yourself! Things like this:

"Look, I'll give it a try, but you know how these things go."
"It's always such drama trying to get a straight answer out of these people..."
"Well, I've come down with the flu, so the whole week's a write-off."

Let's be honest. We live in a world that can be incredibly difficult and trying. There's a lot going on out there, and with a twenty-four-hour news cycle hellbent on reminding everyone of the near-constant catastrophes unfolding all around us, it's no surprise that most people's default setting is a mild (or not-so-mild) pessimism.

But words have power. When you speak, you are not only saying, "This is how the world is," to those around you, you are saying it *yourself*. "This is the way I am."

When Jenna says, "Everyone stays in their own little clique and it's impossible to get to know them," she is actually saying a lot more. She is saying:

The situation cannot be changed, i.e., it's hopeless. She doesn't have any real control over how it plays out, or any agency to change the outcome.
This is true not just for some people, but for all people, including those she hasn't met yet.
Life is largely determined by other people's choices, not her own.
The entire friends-making endeavor is, at its core, a negative experience.

Pretty heavy, huh? Jenna takes all this and carries it with her to every single Meetup and get-together. It impacts her ability to perceive whether people are being kind and friendly to her or not. It changes the way she responds to rejection—or imagined rejection. It alters how she thinks of other people (self-absorbed, kind of mean) and herself (an outsider, passive). In fact, Jenna echoes this very sentiment to someone new she meets at gym one day. "Oh my gosh, it's so nice to finally meet someone *cool*! People in this town can be a little uptight, don't you find?"

Very subtly, she tells the other person exactly what her world is like. Without knowing it, and perhaps without the other person knowing it either, that feeling of hopelessness, negativity, and passivity is quietly shaping her world, and not in good ways. Jenna wants to communicate, "I'm having a hard time meeting people at the moment," and instead communicates, "People don't meet my standards. I'm subtly judging them for not including me." If you were the person in the gym, which attitude would *you* find more attractive and appealing?

Any time we use **"out of power" language, i.e., language that is passive, self-victimizing, doubtful, angry, unconfident, fearful, excuse-making, or pessimistic, we send out powerful messages to ourselves and others. And these messages come back to us**—we can see our attitude reflected to us in the way we feel about ourselves, the way people respond to us, and the way our life is unfolding in general. If all we see and experience is negative, there's a good chance that *we* are the likely common denominator (remember the poisoned pot?).

Habits of speech reflect thought patterns, but in time, they become our choices and actions, and these change and shape our world so that it literally conforms to the thoughts we have about it. This is powerful stuff. Like a sculptor who creates a statue with each scrape of the chisel, you are bit by bit creating your own reality with every word, thought, and action. Luckily for us, though, destructive habits can be identified and replaced.

Try it yourself right now.

It's easy to see the principle in hypothetical Jenna's life—but what does it look like in *yours*? There's a good chance you don't even know. The most damaging and stubborn thought patterns are those that we're not aware of. That means our first task is to become aware of them! You can't look inside your head. But what you can do is monitor your language and infer the contents of your head.

Your **verbal habits** will tell you everything you need to know. <u>For the next twenty-four hours, commit to (neutrally!) observing the language you use to talk to and about yourself.</u> Like a scientist, just gather data for twenty-four hours and refrain from interpreting or judging it.

Notice the words you use, the way you frame things, and the things you *don't* say. Notice the images you use, the subject and object, and, yes, the content, too. Note any assumptions and guesses. What patterns keep appearing?

What to Do about It

Earlier we said that the only things you need to combat negative thinking (or any bad habit) is honest awareness and the willingness to take action—in that order. We will consider many ways to approach both these tasks in later chapters. But for now, see if you can note down in a journal the various verbal habits you've noticed in yourself. Once you do, you can start to gently take action in a different direction.

Everything that is passive is reframed to emphasize your agency and conscious choice. Everything that is imprecise or inaccurate is made specific and realistic. Everything that radiates an energy of hopelessness is replaced with an attitude of mastery, self-command, and purpose. Here's how.

1. *"Reframe forward"*

It's a question of focus. You could talk about what you can't, won't, or don't do, but why not focus instead on what you *can*? You could choose to talk about what isn't working or what you don't like, but why not choose to talk instead about what you love, what excites you, or what you want to create and build?

"I'm an introvert. I hate big crowds," becomes, "I really love one-on-one conversations."

The first is closed, static, and negative; the second is open, alive, and dynamic.

2. Embrace shades of gray

To combat overextrapolating and the all-or-nothing disease, get comfortable with nuance, ambiguity, and degree. Be willing to accept that you are seldom in a position, existentially, to make any all-encompassing statements about the nature of reality. Instead, just be curious and open-ended. This will allow you to take a peek into the "other side" and see what's there . . .

"All the good men are taken," becomes, "I wonder where all the single guys hang out?"
"If a woman hasn't gotten married by forty, it's a red flag, beware!" becomes, "I wonder what kind of person she is and what she cares about."

3. Talk to yourself like you talk to a loved one

Negative self-talk can naturally lead to low self-confidence. Your inner critic is simply the voice of negativity directed at *you* as a person. It's no different from physical self-harm, though. Most of us wouldn't dream of insulting our friends, family, or colleagues, yet we readily do it to ourselves daily. It's one thing to pause and consider if the thought you've just had is accurate, useful, or true. But sometimes, the harm of a thought lies in its *tone*.

Check yourself by **asking if you'd say the same thing to someone you love or even just care about. No? Then don't say it to yourself.** It's not about *what* you say but *how* you say it. If it's rude to deliberately hurt another person's feelings, it's just as bad to hurt your own. Another alternative is to imagine that you're speaking to a little child, or the five-year-old version of yourself. If it seems totally cruel to say to a young, innocent child, then isn't it also cruel to say to yourself?

"You're a nasty fat pig and nobody will love you unless you sort it out already," becomes, "you are overweight, but you're still loved and you deserve support and kindness while you try your best to be better. And you're making real progress every day. Well done!"

Note that framing things in kind, gentle terms doesn't mean lying or ignoring the truth. Many people are suspicious of reframing their thoughts with more kindness because in the past, they have associated "kindness" with "fakeness." It isn't! Rather, it means talking about the truth *with love*.

So, once you've gathered twenty-four hours of data and gained a glimpse into your unique style of talking to yourself, pick a single idea or theme from that data and try to apply the above three approaches. For example:

Recurrent thought: *I hate this job, but I'm stuck doing it if I want to keep paying this stupid mortgage!*

Alternative thought: *It's true that this job isn't a breeze all the time, but I choose to do it because it allows me to pay for a home I love. I'm talented and hardworking, though, so I can always choose to do something else.*

This alternative is "reframed forward" (all about conscious choice and agency: you are not stuck; you love your home), phrased in less absolute terms (the job is difficult, but only some of the time) and with more kindness (focusing on strengths and possibilities). Now you try it!

How to Identify Your Cognitive Distortions

So far, we've spoken of "negative thinking" as though it's all one solid, indistinguishable mass. In the novel *Anna Karenina*, Tolstoy begins with the line: "Happy families are all alike; each unhappy family is unhappy in its own way." It's arguably the same with thought patterns—positivity tends to manifest in a uniform way, whereas there seem to be about a million ways for thoughts to be "negative"!

In the last chapter, you monitored your thought processes for just one day and worked on reframing a single thought or idea that stood out to you. In this chapter, we'll continue on this path and take a closer look at some of the kinds of negativity we're likely to encounter when we pay attention to our "thought traffic." In other words, if negativity is a distortion of reality, then this distortion can manifest in several different forms. Learn to identify these forms, and you'll become better at spotting distortions rather than being taken in by them.

A cognitive distortion is an incorrect belief, perception, or thought.

Of course, nobody is perfect and infallible, and we're all wrong sometimes, but *persistently* distorted cognition is a problem—and it's about a lot more than simply being "right" or "wrong."

Where do these distortions come from? For the time being, assume that every mental twist and warp served a purpose at one time. Typically, distortions help us overcome trauma or loss in the past—however, if they continue long after the threat has passed, they tend to undermine rather than protect us.

Crucially, it does not really matter where these distortions come from. Trying to analyze *why* you think the way you do is a little like being shot with an arrow and then sitting down, in agony, wondering which direction the arrow came from and who shot it and why. There's no need! Just pull the arrow out, and you will instantly feel better. This is why, in this book, we won't spend too much time delving into the past, because, after all, that's not where the trouble is. What matters is how you think here and now. Why a belief started is less important than how you're *sustaining* it right now.

We've already explored one major and very common distortion: **all-or-nothing thinking**. This is when we overextrapolate and break the complex world down into two either/or polar extremes and force ourselves to pick one of them (a decision we don't notice that we *ourselves* have insisted on). This kind of distortion is characterized (but not *always*—

ha!) by absolutist terms like *always*, *never*, *everyone*, *none*, etc.

"If you don't agree with me, then you're part of the problem."

"If I don't get into college, my life is ruined."

Or, for that matter: "Either I think positively, or I think negatively."

Let's look at some more distortions you may uncover as you gain awareness.

Mental Filtering

This is basically like having a sieve in your head that only allows you to perceive and engage with certain data, while whatever doesn't "fit" is allowed to pass right through as though it doesn't exist. Once you're done filtering, the only things left in the sieve are those things that align with the preconceived worldview you started with.

Consider the example of Carrie, who has a severely distorted idea of what she looks like (sadly, all too common in a world that stands to gain by her insecurities). Carrie goes out shopping for clothing one day and enters the changing rooms of several different stores. Three of the four mirrors reflect a fairly flattering image, while the final place she visits is a store with extremely poor light.

Carrie gets home after the shopping trip and says, "Well, that was a waste of time! I don't know why I thought I'd find anything that looks half decent on me . . ." She completely forgets about the three flattering changing rooms and only remembers the one where she *didn't* look good. Her mental sieve is shaped in such a way as to catch and collect all those experiences that align with the conclusion she has already come to about herself—she is unattractive—and completely disregards anything that challenges this conclusion.

In Carrie's world, it's as though those flattering reflections never even existed. If a friend points this out, she might reply, "Yeah, sure, but those mirrors artificially make people look better so you buy their clothes!" In other words, Carrie's distortion is this: Only the negative is true or to be focused on; the positive is insignificant or an illusion. This is connected to another distortion that's called "disqualifying the positive." Here, we may be aware of data that doesn't fit the preconceived idea, but we make up some story about why that data doesn't matter.

"Oh, it was just a lucky break/beginner's luck."

"The ten times I've succeeded so far were just a fluke; this most recent time that I failed was the real deal. That was all me."

"People don't mean it. They're being polite/kind/their opinions don't count."

If Carrie's friend says, "You forgot about all those lovely dresses we tried on earlier and how nice you looked in them!" Carrie might say, "Well, you would say that because you're sweet and you're my friend." In fact, Carrie might go as far as to find something negative *in* the positive, secretly thinking, "I bet she pities me and is just trying to make me feel better by pretending I look better than I do. It must be even worse than I thought!"

Later in this book, we'll look at how Carrie's tendency, although extreme, is actually a fairly common phenomenon called "negativity bias," which has evolutionary roots.

Personalization

Mental shortcuts and biases exist because the brain is trying to explain to itself *why* something happens, and to make sense of events. Call it an existential self-centeredness, but human beings can sometimes imagine that random things have more to do with them personally than they actually do. In the realm of negative thinking, this can look like assuming that anything negative must be somehow your fault or reflect poorly on you.

While filtering can make you zoom in on the negative or imagine that it's there when it isn't, personalization is where **you perceive a genuine negative but incorrectly ascribe its cause or source as yourself**. It's as though you say, "There's a bad thing over there, and I'm a bad thing over here . . . so we must belong together somehow."

One day, Carrie goes to a friend's wedding and is obsessing all morning about whether the outfit she has chosen looks okay. When she gets to the event, the friend is hurried and busy and says in a lighthearted way, "Well, we haven't had any disasters yet, but let's just say not everybody seems to know what *semi-formal* means these days, if you know what I mean . . ."

Carrie immediately thinks that this comment is aimed at her and that her friend is implying that she isn't dressed properly. In other words, she has correctly noticed the stress and fluster of her friend, but has incorrectly ascribed the cause to herself, passing it again through the same filter, which only ever allows one conclusion: You look awful. Similarly, when Carrie's boyfriend cheats on her later that year, she doesn't skip a beat before concluding that he has done so because the other woman was better looking.

(In case you're wondering, the personalization bias can go the other way, where we find ourselves taking credit for things that have nothing to do with us, but this is usually less common! The most common and subtle way to personalize neutral stimuli is simply to assume that we're the center of the universe, and to find ways to refer every external event back to ourselves. We tend to do this in a way that confirms our other existing biases. So, for example, someone might tell Carrie they're feeling depressed, and Carrie might assume, "They probably hate the way they look.")

Jumping to Conclusions and Mind-Reading

Closely related to the above distortion is the tendency to **make assumptions about other people's intentions and motivations, in the absence of any evidence**. Carrie automatically assumes that she is the only one at the wedding that the friend could possibly be referring to, and also assumes that her own mental filter exists in her boyfriend's head, too, who couldn't think anything else but, "Carrie is unattractive." **Mindreading is unconsciously filling in the blanks and assuming that others' thought processes must broadly be in alignment with**

our own. This is easy to do when you consider how infrequently we stop to actually communicate and check what people really are thinking!

In fact, rather than thinking about the situation from many perspectives, Carrie weaves an elaborate tale in her head about his cheating: He finds her unattractive and always has, and as soon as someone better looking came along, he went for her . . . and who can blame him? In assuming that his cheating is purely to do with her, Carrie is not just personalizing but mindreading. Without having a stitch of evidence, she "knows" that he thinks this. Her distortion blinds her to a more likely interpretation: Her boyfriend cheated because he's a dishonest and disloyal person. Or he's immature and made a foolish mistake. Or, just maybe, he himself has no idea why he acted as he did . . .

Catastrophizing

Also known as magnification or minimization, depending on which direction your distortion wants to go! Basically, this is **the tendency to exaggerate**. Carrie never says she's *plain* or *average looking* but full-on *hideous*. She's not just unattractive, but the most unattractive person who ever lived. And the fact that she's hideous also implies the worst possible outcome, namely that nobody will ever love her and that she's doomed to an ugly, lonely life where small children burst into tears upon seeing her in the street.

Minimization can be just as distorting as magnification, though. Carrie could spend an hour getting ready one morning, doing her hair, fixing her makeup, and dressing in beautiful clothing, only to announce at the end of it, "It makes zero difference; I still look the same."

Negative thinkers tend to exaggerate the size of a threat while, at the same time, downplaying their own resilience, their resources, their strength, and their ability to cope with that threat, real or imagined. The negative gets amplified and carried to extremes, while the glimmer of hope is reduced to nothing.

Carrie sits alone one evening and imagines that her life is over. The negativity around her appearance has become so all-encompassing that it takes on the feeling of a catastrophe. It doesn't matter that she has a fascinating job, lots of caring friends, a happy family, and countless talents and interests. The perceived faults in her appearance are magnified so much that they eclipse all these things and reduce them to insignificance while she sits to the side, completely powerless to stop any of it.

"Shoulds" and Labels

Here's where it gets interesting for Carrie. When she starts becoming more aware of her own thought patterns and habitual negativity, she realizes that much of her perception comes from comparing herself against an idea of what she *should* look like. Her hair is wavy and fluffy—but it should be straight and silky. She is on the taller side, but she *should* be more petite. Her eyes are black when they *should* be blue or green or at least hazel.

Now, this book is not about to ask where Carrie got all these expectations from (although most of us can probably guess). Instead, it's about the fact that comparison against some real or imaginary standard is so often the source of negativity. Many of us are perfectly happy with our lot . . . right up until we start to see how we measure up against everyone else. Only then do we feel a lack.

Closely related to this is the idea of labels. We can think of labels as a whole collection of "shoulds" that have coalesced into one. The label "beautiful woman" is then a checklist of shoulds. A beautiful woman must be X, she must be Y, and she must be Z. This is not reality, however, but an arbitrary rule we create about reality . . . and then we suffer because we don't align with that rule. If you doubt this, consider how all the women with straight hair would love to have curls, and all the women with curly hair would love for it to be straight!

If Carrie's example seems superficial to you, then consider something a little more serious. Imagine that Carrie's friends are all intelligent, successful, and independent young women who are more than aware of the burden of beauty standards and the effect they have on mental health. One day, she opens up and says that she has always hated her appearance and wishes more than anything that she could look like those beautiful women she sees in social media.

How do these friends respond? They dismiss it. "You should love yourself! You shouldn't pay attention to that garbage, and anyway, physical appearances don't matter. People should value one another for what's on the inside." Sounds nice. But it's also a kind of cognitive distortion. Clearly, appearances *do* matter. Instead of making Carrie feel better, this is the kind of thing that's likely to make her feel worse—not only is she now unhappy about her appearance because she *should* look prettier, she's now also unhappy about her own unhappiness because she *should* be confident and self-accepting enough not to care . . .

Comparing against some assumed normal or correct standard is a little like arguing with reality. Sometimes, we put ourselves in the role of CEO of the universe, there to unilaterally decide what happens and when, putting labels on things according to our own (flawed) understanding. So we say things like, "A beautiful woman is supposed to be dainty and small," or, "A confident woman shouldn't have those kinds of insecurities." *Says who?* When you say "should," then what usually follows is a judgment—usually not in your favor!

As you can see, a really juicy cognitive distortion doesn't limit itself—it can be all of the above and more! Carrie's distortions are a complex cocktail of a range of different biases and assumptions. But each of them is working in the same way, reinforcing a negative worldview and completely destroying the chance of arriving at a more realistic, healthy one.

But consider this: What would happen if Carrie's mind wasn't working so hard to undermine her at every turn? What if instead, its powers of critical thinking, conscious awareness, and intelligent choice let her live a completely different kind of life? Once you've identified your cognitive distortions and seen all the many ways they can show up in your stream of self-talk, then you're going to naturally start wondering... what does life look like *without* all these distortions?

How to Challenge Your Inner Critic

You don't need a formal introduction to your inner critic—you are well acquainted and have probably heard from it several times already today! This is the "voice" inside that criticizes, judges, and condemns. Your anti-cheerleader.

"You're doing it wrong."
"That's nowhere near good enough."
"Everyone's talking about you."
"You may as well just give up."
"Who do you think you are?"
We've looked at a few ways to reframe your perspective, embrace shades of gray, and adjust how you speak to yourself so it's closer to how you'd speak to a loved one. But a funny thing happens once you start paying attention to your inner critic—it starts to feel like it's *everywhere*! Now what?

Step 1: See thoughts as thoughts

This is the most important step. When your inner critic says, "This is hopeless," you hear it, but you can say to yourself, "My inner critic is telling me that it's hopeless." Big difference. Your negative self-talk is not reality. Simply remind yourself of this and you've drastically reduced its power over you. Your thoughts are just thoughts. They come; they go.

Step 2: Gain distance

Make it really obvious to your brain that these are thoughts and that they are separate from reality and from who you really are at your core. Give your inner critic a name. Maybe imagine that it's literally an annoying little bug standing in the corner, trying to get a rise out of you. There's an enormous shift in perspective when you go from, "Everything is hopeless and terrible," to, "Look at that, here's the Depression Fairy again coming to visit. Hey, Mildred, how are you doing?"

Step 3: Be compassionate

One temptation is to rail against the inner critic when you find it. You might want to argue viciously against it or perhaps feel shame that it's there at all. Resist this temptation. Instead, treat the inner critic with civility, attention, and kindness. Imagine yourself pulling up a chair at the table and feeding your inner critic a meal just the same as you would your inner defender. When we are compassionate, we normalize negativity and take away its sting. "You're feeling sad right now. That's okay. You do feel sad sometimes, but you've also had lots of joyful experiences, too."

Step 4: Do nothing

Yes, really! This one is easy—refuse to act while guided by your inner critic. It can be a passenger in the car, but it certainly doesn't get to drive! We can't always help how we feel, but we *can* make conscious choices about how we act and what we say. Own that power. Refuse to act from your inner critic—act instead from that part of you that is aware, healthy, and realistic. "Yes, Mildred, I know you want to pick a fight right now, but instead, we're going for a walk!"

What Positive Self-Talk Actually Looks Like

Positive self-talk is not just the absence of negative distortions. It has its own quality and character, and you'll know what these are by the way you feel when you talk to yourself in this way: calm, hopeful, curious, grateful, stable, confident.

Positive self-talk doesn't mean we are constantly giving ourselves an over-the-top pep talk about how utterly fabulous we are—this is, after all, just another distortion. Rather, there is a kind of **dignified willingness to face reality as it is, and the confidence that comes with owning your free will and acting in ways that align with your values.**

So, when something unexpected and unpleasant crops up, you think, "Huh, look at that! This is going to be challenging, but I wonder how I can get around it? I'm not sure yet, but I'll find a way." When something new and promising pops up, you look it square in the eye and say, "Wow, I never thought about this before—let's follow it and see what happens!"

Positive thinking is not just *content*—it's *feeling*. As you get into the habit of pausing to notice what's in your head, don't just look at the concepts; look at your attitude and emotional state. This will also help you avoid the common pitfall of "toxic positivity"—approaching your positive self-talk from a place of anxiety, self-hate, and avoidance!

In your comfort zone is the way you've tended to always think, and outside of it is the way you could think—a potentially better way. Separating the two is a line, which at some point, if you want to evolve, you have to cross. If you've been a negative thinker for a long time, your automatic response to everything we've explored so far might be, "Sounds fine, but that will never work for me," or, "That's too simple; the real world is a lot more complicated!"

The thing is, before we go any further, be aware that at some point, **you have to take a leap of faith and cross that line—even if you don't have evidence yet that it will work**. All the positive affirmations and mindfulness exercises in the world will do nothing if you're making the unconscious decision to never cross that line.

<u>Before we move to the next chapter, challenge yourself to one final exercise</u>.

For the next twenty-four hours, *act as if* you are a person who thinks positively all the time. It doesn't matter if you believe it or not yet, just try it out and, for twenty-four hours only, let go of any doubts and suspicions. Bring a sense of humor to it, if you want to. Then, at the end of the twenty-four hours, pay attention to how you feel.

Once you can actually **feel for yourself**, in your own experience, the power of positive thinking, you will no longer be engaging with the techniques and exercises on a purely superficial level. You will no longer be satisfied with staying on this side of the line, only peeking over to the other side without ever taking the leap.

Summary
- How you think creates your life; negativity poisons everything in your world.
- Changing negativity requires a degree of metacognition (thinking about thinking) and a leap of faith to do something that hasn't been done before. Anyone can change their thought patterns; it requires only honest awareness and a willingness to take conscious and inspired action.
- Our mental shortcuts, assumptions, biases, and stereotypes are great at saving time and effort, but are not one hundred percent accurate one hundred percent of the time. The "all-or-nothing" disease is when we overextrapolate from one experience to other experiences we haven't had; we are making an error.
- Words have power, and our speech reflects our thought patterns. "Out of power" language is passive, self-victimizing, doubtful, angry, unconfident, fearful, excuse-making, or pessimistic, and can create a self-fulfilling prophesy.
- Become aware of your internal verbal habits. Then focus on what can be done, embrace nuance and shades of gray, and speak to yourself like you would a loved one.

- A cognitive distortion is a persistently incorrect belief, perception, or thought—for example, mental filtering, personalization, jumping to conclusions, mind-reading, catastrophizing, and using "should" statements and labels.
- Positive thinking is not just the absence of distortions, but thinking that helps you feel calm, hopeful, curious, grateful, stable, and confident.
- To challenge your inner critic, commit to not allowing your thoughts to dominate you. Gain psychological distance by labeling the thoughts as thoughts, not reality, and have self-compassion.
- Change happens outside your comfort zone, so realize that at some point, you'll need to take the leap and try something new.

Chapter 2: Analyze Thyself: the ABC Method and Thought Journals

We've explored the idea of reframing thoughts, and began to identify cognitive distortions as well as gently challenge them as they emerge. It's important that we have these fundamental paradigm shifts in place *first*; otherwise, we will merely be working **within** our negative mindset, not working **on** our negative mindset. As Einstein famously said, "We can't solve problems by using the same kind of thinking we used when we created them."

In this chapter, we'll look more closely at a concrete technique for **slowing right down and rewriting the very programming that our negative thinking runs on.**

But first, let's look at the insights gathered by the founder of cognitive behavioral therapy (CBT), Albert Ellis. In his work, he couldn't help but notice that different people seemed to respond very differently to similar events. Why? The events themselves didn't explain the difference—it must be the thoughts, feelings, and beliefs of the people who were *interpreting* these events. Over the years, Ellis came to the same conclusion that Shakespeare arguably did in *Hamlet* when he said, **"There is nothing either good or bad, but thinking makes it so."**

Thoughts, feelings, and actions are all connected and work together to create your response to external events. The ABC method, inspired by this understanding, helps us tease apart the different elements:

A is for activating event. This is neutral in the sense that it only takes on meaning and value according to our response to it.

B is for beliefs. How we respond internally to the event.

C is for consequence.

Importantly, the outcome (consequence) is not a direct result of the event, but of our *interpretation* of the event. The event is always neutral. You can see where this is going: If we want to change our lives, we shouldn't start with A, the external events, but B, how we think about the events these events come from.

The way that each of us responds to Event A is wholly a matter of conditioned response and association. To put it simply, we've *learned* to respond to activating events in very particular ways. Again, these associations are neutral. It's the resulting consequences that make the difference. If we find that our conditioned responses are continually undermining our effectiveness and wellbeing, then we can take action to adjust things—noting, of course, that the adjustment has to happen with the relationship between A and B, and not at C, which is really just a symptom of our conditioning and not the problem itself.

In CBT, the goal is to make adaptive changes, so two new letters are added:

D is for disputation. This is where we challenge the ideas in B.

E is for new effect. Something different to replace the old C.

Let's look at an example. Dan has always loved motorcycles and owns several. One fateful day, he is out riding at night and has an accident: He collides with a car, severely injuring the mother and daughter inside, totaling his favorite bike and leaving him with spinal damage that means that he will not ride a bike again for years—if ever. That's one big, gnarly activating event!

Believe it or not, Ellis would say that this event, tragic as it appears, is neutral and has no meaning by itself. But Dan is right there and responding instantly: He is completely destroyed with guilt and remorse. He calls it a tragedy. His world is so shaken by the event that he considers it a pivotal moment—before the accident, he was happy, carefree, and innocent. After it, he was a condemned man, miserable, doomed to carry the remorse of the damage he'd caused—not to mention the physical pain from his own significant injuries.

Dan refuses to forgive himself. Despite being forgiven by the mother and the daughter in the car, and despite everyone around him telling him that it was an accident and not his fault, Dan is eaten up with shame and the deep wish to turn back time. He falls into a depression and, perhaps unconsciously, starts to punish himself. He withdraws socially and stops taking care of himself. A pattern of self-defeating, negative thinking seeps into his world.

Here's how the ABC method applies to Dan:

A – The activating event is the accident.

B – There are many beliefs here, but the big one is, "I am guilty. I'm a bad, bad person."

C – The consequences are obvious. Dan spirals into depression and self-loathing, unable to forgive himself or move on.

Now, the ABC part of the model is a roadmap to help explain the relationship between thoughts, feelings, and behavior. But it's only when Dan seeks therapy with a CBT psychologist that he is asked to add on the other two letters and work through this dynamic so it can be transformed.

Filled with grief and distress, Dan enters therapy and wants to talk about the details of the gruesome accident. The therapist listens, but he is not interested so much in the details of the story as he is in the meaning underneath them— he listens for the *beliefs* that inform the way Dan talks about his experience. Dan uses plenty of cognitive distortions (catastrophizing, "should" statements, and a heaping dose of personalization), but the therapist doesn't engage with these—instead, he becomes curious about the core beliefs that these distortions are serving.

They work together, and Dan becomes aware of the story he is telling himself about the event.

Simply realizing he is telling a story in the first place allows him to gain some distance and perspective (more on this in the next section). The therapist starts to gently challenge Dan—**is there possibly a different way of looking at the whole thing?** Seeing clearly how the current story is damaging his life, Dan agrees he has nothing to lose and that he will try out a different perspective:

"It was a sad and regrettable accident, but I did not do it on purpose. It's true that I am responsible for the pain caused, but I never intended to hurt anyone, and that means that I am *not* a bad person, but just a person who made a mistake. Carrying shame and guilt doesn't serve anyone, including me. It's okay that I have found this difficult, but I can also give myself permission to move on now and live my life again."

So, is that the "right" story? Maybe. Dan could also tell another one:

"The day of the accident was the worst day of my life. But despite all the pain, I am grateful it happened because it taught me something precious: to never take anything for granted, to live while I can, and to appreciate every moment I have. That means going out there and living life in the best way I possibly can so that when it's my time to die, I know I've lived well and will not be filled with regret."

Completely different story. In fact, there are probably an infinite number of stories to tell about this event. None of them are right or wrong. However, all of them will lead to particular consequences. Are those consequences in line with a happy, healthy life that we want to create for ourselves? *That's* how we tell if a story is one we want to adopt.

Often, CBT is simply presented as a way to make simple and superficial tweaks to single sentences—for example, instead of saying, "This is hard; I can't do it," you say, "This is challenging, but I'll try my best." Make no mistake, this sort of alteration *is* incredibly helpful. It's just that, in real life, you've probably noticed that your problems tend to take the form of stories rather than simple, discrete statements.

You can use the principles of CBT in your own life. By using a "thought journal," you can carefully work through the three elements (event, belief, and consequence) and start to replace destructive or unhelpful beliefs with better ones. Before we look at that, though, here's a note on what "better" looks like when it comes to thoughts.

No, they don't have to be relentlessly "positive." But a good replacement will be:

- **Accurate** – it is a close reflection of external reality
- **Helpful** – it actually assists you in achieving what you want in your life
- **Congruent** – it aligns with who you are and the values and principles you hold dear. It goes without saying, but the thoughts you use to replace unhelpful ones shouldn't be simply copied and pasted from someone else's life—they have to genuinely mean something to *you*.

Being your own CBT therapist is a little like applying the Find and Replace function on Microsoft Word. There are two parts. First, observe and identify your thoughts. Second, rewrite these beliefs and allow the change in perception to filter through to your actions and behaviors in the external world. Then, take note of the results, adjust, and repeat!

One warning: try to remember that you are not psychoanalyzing yourself. If Dan started to unpick his childhood and unravel his relationship with his mother and came to some lofty and complicated ideas about how the motorcycle is really a phallic symbol representing his masculine id, and how the accident was really a manifestation of his repressed rage and an unconscious ploy to castrate his father, who was simultaneously cruel but masochistic... then this is just another story. A weird one.

At best it's a distraction from real improvement; at worst it might more deeply embed certain harmful beliefs into Dan's mind. Remember that your task is not forensic and is not based in the past. You are not required to construct an interesting-sounding theory about why things have happened as they have. Instead, just keep focused on the response you are having to neutral stimuli.

What are the consequences? What can you change to arrive at consequences you like more? That's all there is to it.

Step 1: How to Keep a Thought Journal

This is not a conventional journal in the sense that you simply sit down and write whatever comes to you. While doing so has some therapeutic value, you'll want to be a little more focused and deliberate when keeping a thought journal. You're trying to understand:

What are the main events that have occurred in my life?

What are the beliefs I hold about these events?

What are the emotions that result from thinking this way?

How do I act and behave because I hold this belief?

A thought journal can be used in a non-directed way if you merely want to gain some self-knowledge, but it's best used when there is a particular problem you're working through. Sit down when you won't be disturbed, and give yourself five or ten minutes to just explore how you think and feel. Put it all down on paper—it doesn't have to be perfect or make sense. Hold it all loosely and don't try to interpret anything just yet. After the time is up, you may choose to take a little break before looking at it again.

When you look again, you may notice some patterns and themes emerging. Maybe you go back through the text and pull these out with a highlighter. Or maybe you allow the main ideas and thoughts to coalesce into a few sentences. You'll probably notice a few cognitive distortions in the mix!

As you're writing or re-reading, don't try to avoid painful or uncomfortable themes—in fact, lean into those, as they will most reliably lead you to your core beliefs about the event that's underway. Try also to avoid making any pronouncements just yet—don't let that inner critic weigh in with judgments and diagnoses. Give yourself permission just to honestly express everything—yes, even that thing you're trying hard not to think about! In the beginning, it's just about curiosity.

Let's look at an example: Carl's boss has alerted him to an industry conference that he'd be willing to pay for—if Carl can come up with a good presentation. Carl's anxiety instantly goes through the roof. He sits down to journal it out, slowing his thought processes so he can get a handle on them.

As best he can, he tries to write down a neutral, objective account of events: He's been asked to do a presentation. He's never done one before. What beliefs does he hold? He just writes them down before he can second-guess himself: *I'm not good enough. My boss thinks I'm more able than I am. I hate public speaking. This is going to be humiliating . . .* What emotions does he feel? There are the obvious ones: fear, panic, self-loathing. But he also identifies another feeling—it's almost like tiredness, like the anticipation of being overwhelmed.

He looks more closely at this feeling, and it reveals another, quite hidden belief he has: If I succeed at this, then I'll have to keep on doing it, and I'm not sure I want to. Seeing this, he realizes he's felt this way before: that if he succeeds, then people will come to expect that from him, holding him to higher standards, and his life will suddenly get harder and more demanding. Because he thinks and feels this way, his behavior suddenly makes more sense to him: He feels avoidant and noncommittal and says yes to the conference, but only out of a sense of duty.

Teasing all these feelings apart is not just an academic exercise—finding out his *exact* thought patterns around this issue will allow Carl to make the best of the next step. After all, if you saw the problem as low self-belief, it would suggest a different solution than if you saw the problem as a lack of alignment with values, or even burnout. Take some time with your own issue, and don't rush it. There may be several layers to your ingrained thought patterns!

Step 2: Rethink . . . and Redo
Once you've identified the key thought patterns and core beliefs hiding inside your current situation, it's time to **get curious about alternative ways of looking at things**. Once you've done that, then the next step becomes

obvious, too: You **think of ways to implement those new beliefs via action**.

It might be helpful to summarize things neatly by creating a table of two columns. One column is the negative thought pattern you currently hold, and the other column is where you brainstorm new beliefs and interpretations. The key point about this exercise, though, is that *intellectually* understanding what a better alternative would look like does not mean that you instantly replace it. Chances are, your negative thought patterns have been there for a while—it will take time to experience a genuine and lasting shift to something different, so be patient and realistic.

In Carl's case, he narrows down his beliefs on this issue to a few key thoughts:

I am only allowed to do the work I'm good at.

I can't let people down, even if living up to their expectations makes me really unhappy.

If an opportunity comes along, you have to take it because you never know if you'll get another one.

Carl recognizes that versions of these beliefs have popped up all throughout his life. He brainstorms a few realistic alternatives that he feels he can live with:

Just because I do well at something, it doesn't mean that I'm committed to doing it forever.

People's expectations of me are their own business, and I am not "letting anyone down" by doing what is right for me.

I can face any new opportunity with curiosity and gratitude, but I can also take the time to decide whether it aligns with my goals.

However, writing something new in the second column is the very least you can do. You have to imagine really drilling this new way of thinking into your mind—it has to become *real* for you. There are many ways of doing this, but passively waiting for your mind to catch up is not likely to work. This is where action can help. Imagine that everything you write in the second column is purely hypothetical—that is, until you take action to make it real.

Here are a few ideas:

- **Take action that supplies you with evidence that supports your new belief**. Your brain is intelligent—it doesn't want to believe something without proof. So, in Carl's example, his unhelpful thought is, "I am obligated to deliver on every expectation people have of me." He can put it to the test. In a small way, he can refuse to let someone else's expectations determine the action he will take. Or, for a bigger step, he can tell his boss he is attending a conference—but a different one that is more aligned with his interests and expertise. When the boss is okay with this and the world doesn't actually end, Carl can make a mental note—maybe his beliefs are not as accurate as he thought. Then he can take another small step. Gradually, he is accumulating evidence for his new belief: *"People's expectations of me are their own business, and I am not 'letting anyone down' by doing what is right for me."*

- **Create and strengthen a new filter.** Your old mental filter worked hard to only notice those things that confirmed your core belief. Every day, pause to deliberately ask yourself to look at things in a way that aligns with your new belief. For example, the old thought "I get depressed in winter" will give way to the new one "There are many things about winter that I still enjoy" if you try to find five things you love about each winter day when you wake up. In Carl's case, he can gradually start to build a filter that reframes people's expectations of him not as demands, but as genuinely interesting *opportunities and possibilities*—ones he is always at liberty to appraise as he sees fit. And when people communicate their expectations and hopes for him, he can filter this so their excitement is interpreted as care and kindness. He can slowly learn to respond to this good intention, rather than getting stressed that it means that he suddenly has to perform or else.

- **Practice self-compassion**. Remember that cognitive distortions are not only about *content*, but about *feeling*. You might find that your thought processes are fairly rational and realistic, but the problem is that they're just too harsh! For example, the thought, "Most of my life is behind me," may be literally true . . . but it's kind of unflattering. Here, taking action may simply mean being brave enough to face what's uncomfortable with humor and kindness. "Well, you can't go on an epic journey without putting a few miles on the clock!" Be polite and courteous to yourself. A little tact goes a long way. Try a handy trick for quickly cultivating self-acceptance: Put the words ". . . and I love that" at the end of something you're framing as a problem. "I failed my driver's test . . . and

I love that." It's not a magic wand, but isn't it interesting how it shifts your perspective? Maybe it's not the end of the world that you're flawed or struggling in the way you are. At least consider the possibility.

In Carl's case, a little compassion could remind him that he is entitled to seek out work he values and to be a little easier on himself. He may find out, in fact, that his boss actually has no big expectation of how the conference will go and was only making a suggestion—all of the pressure was coming from Carl alone.

- **Change statements to questions**. Your core beliefs are just that—beliefs, not facts. If you find in the first column the thought, "Nobody wants to hire someone with my skills." Change it to, "*Is* anyone hiring someone with my skills?" Literally go and check! Sounds too simple, but we often allow assumptions to act like facts in our lives. Be curious. Don't say how the door is closed—ask about any other doors around you that *are* open. In fact, while you're at it, ask about secret escape routes hidden under the floor you're standing on! Carl could simply come out and ask his boss, "If I really do well at this conference, do you envision asking me to make more presentations in the future?" Imagine all the stress that Carl could avoid if the boss says, "Not at all. I just thought you might enjoy it."

- **Go into learning mode**. A great trick is to ask yourself "how?" Instead of saying, "I can't do this," say, "How can I do this?" If something isn't working, don't focus on that fact—ask what *does* work. If you have the belief, "I'll always be bad with money," then combat it with a very concrete, realistic question: "How can I start to improve my financial literacy?" This way, you're not getting hung up on the fact of a challenge or obstacle, you're just skipping right over it and refusing to dwell—instead, asking what happens next. One very powerful question to ask, no matter what you're struggling with, is, "What kind of person do I have to be right now to cope with this well?"

For Carl, a great way to get out of his particular thought pattern is to ask, "What do I expect of myself? If I don't like making presentations, then what do I like doing? How can I do more of that at work?"

Decenter, Shift Perspective, and Create Distance

Meet Chris. It's Monday morning, and just as Chris gets into his car to make the daily commute to work, he notices a red light flashing on the dashboard. He swears under his breath and drives to work anyway, trying to ignore the warning bell, but with a sinking feeling in his gut that this means a big nasty bill that he won't be able to avoid. He gets to work after sitting in traffic for a while and is immediately met with a message that a client has submitted a complaint about him. His boss wants to chat. At the same moment, he realizes that he's forgotten his wallet at home and hasn't brought any lunch with him.

When a colleague peeks her head around the door and asks if he's okay, he says, not really joking, "Just kill me now please." She asks what the problem is, and he says, "I don't know, *life*?" The colleague mentions that she wanted to ask him a few questions about a funding request he submitted last week, and he quips, "Oh yeah? What's wrong with it? Let me guess, I've made a mistake and have to spend ninety years in prison for fraud? Or wait, I've got it. They've done the calculations and *I* actually owe *them* money, right?"

The colleague mutters something and scuttles off. Chris sits fuming in his office and all at once feels like crying. He hates himself for it, but whenever an unexpected expense comes up, he finds himself panicking. He remembers how his mom and dad struggled financially and battled to keep their beat-up old car running, once or twice having to forfeit the heating bill or that week's groceries to pay for an unexpected repair.

Here's something that many people seldom think about: **Pessimism, negativity, and gloomy nihilism are all coping mechanisms**. It might not look like it, but these responses signal that at some point, you came to the conclusion that your best bet was not to expect too much from life and instead be ready to assume the worst. This kind of negative attitude is a coping mechanism . . . but it's certainly not a good one. That's because it disempowers you and tends to more firmly entrench the things that are oppressing you, rather than enable you to rise above them.

When you begin to shift your thinking to a more positive direction, you may be taking away the only coping mechanism that is protecting you from experiencing a whole world of pain, hurt, disappointment, anger, and fear. Luckily, though, we don't have to live in the world without coping mechanisms—we can choose better, healthier ones.

*Sh*t Happens . . . Even if You Think Positively*

There is a perhaps unconscious assumption that if only you learn to master the fine art of positive thinking, your life will somehow be much, much easier. This may be true, but only in the sense that with positive thinking, **you become more resilient and better able to cope**—positive thinking, it should be said, doesn't magically make your life completely free of adversity. It doesn't remove challenging events but gives you a different way of responding to them.

Most of us are able to maintain a sunny disposition for a while (i.e., as long as nothing goes too wrong!), but we falter when we encounter our old wounds and traumas, the unfairness of life, a painful loss, or a moment of genuine confusion and chaos. The irony is that these moments are when we need positive thinking the most.

In the previous chapters, we looked at fixing our relationship with our own minds and making sure that we weren't deliberately undermining ourselves with destructive and distorted thought patterns. But, as any good pessimist would point out, they are negative for a *reason*!

Those reasons are seemingly infinite: unexpected car repairs, complaints and conflicts, silly misunderstandings, and accidents . . .

We cannot avoid a degree of friction in life. And we certainly can do nothing about things that have already happened in the past. But how can we cope with it in a calmer and more measured way? What does a healthy coping mechanism look like? Let's bear in mind that sh*t happens even if you think positively. The trick is to accept this fact and find a good way to manage it.

How to Take a Step Back
Think about Chris's colleague in the example above. She comes in, chats with him for a moment, and then quickly decides to retreat. Why? Probably because she can tell what a foul mood he's in! She knows there's no use engaging when he's so grumpy, so she doesn't. She physically removes herself from the room. We're considering the colleague only because she is able to do something that Chris, in that moment, cannot: gain distance. She can observe the behavior as it unfolds and realize that it's temporary. But Chris is stuck right in it, completely at its mercy.

When you gain psychological distance, what you are doing is taking a deep breath,

stepping back from the situation, and becoming a temporary observer rather than a wholly enmeshed and identified participant.

With psychological distance, you are able to step out of the narrow tunnel of your immediate experience and look at the bigger picture. Had Chris been able to do this, he might have said to himself or his colleague, "Look, I'm having a difficult morning and I'm stressing a little about money. It's okay and it will pass, but before I do anything further, I just want to wait until I've calmed down a bit."

Here are a few other techniques that Chris could have tried.

Create Spatial Distance

Literally separate yourself from the problem—go outside and take a walk if the place you're in is overwhelming, or write worrying thoughts in a journal and make a ritual of setting this journal in a locked drawer in another room—i.e., where it's far away from you. Perhaps Chris imagines physical space—he meditates for a few moments where he visualizes himself in a peaceful faraway garden where he can gather his thoughts for a moment.

Create Temporal Distance

We can take a step away from difficult experiences not just in space, but in time. Think about how this situation will look to you in one, two, or ten years' time. Can you think of a similar challenging situation that happened in the past? How do you feel about it now that some time has passed? Did any of your fears come true? How did you cope? Have you actually evolved and learned new ways of coping since then?

Chris zooms out—way out—and visualizes himself on his death bed. He feels calmer as he realizes that life was indeed filled with annoying crises that came and went, but that they mean absolutely nothing in the grand scheme!

The next time you're struggling with something, gain distance by imagining your future self in ten years' time. Then, as your future self, answer the following questions:

- What do you think about the current issue?
- What is your stress rating of the issue compared to the stress rating your current self is experiencing (on a scale of 1 to 10)?
- What do you know that your current self doesn't know?

Another way to do this exercise is to think to the past and a stressful event that happened then. Ask yourself these questions:

- How distressed were you (on a scale from 1 to 10)? At what rating did the feeling peak?
- How long did the feeling last?
- When and how did it stop?

Play with Role-Switching

What would other people do in your shoes? Think of someone you respect and admire, and imagine the problem through their eyes. This helps separate you from your own blind spots and tender points. Chris has a lot of traumatic memories from his childhood, but he always loved and revered his father. He thinks about how his dad was tough and no-nonsense about practical problems and would say, "To hell with it! I'll learn to fix it myself." This inspires Chris because it reminds him of his own resourcefulness.

Another possibility is to imagine your Higher Self, whatever that looks like to you. Some people may like to imagine a deity, a guardian angel, or a supernatural being who provides sagely guidance. If an all-knowing, wise, and loving entity looked with interest at your current problem, what would they advise you to do? If that doesn't feel authentic to you, imagine a personal hero or role model and how they'd respond—even if they're fictional!

Focus on Concrete Action

When Chris is having his Monday morning meltdown, he isn't thinking clearly, to put it bluntly. His distress and anxiety is like an amorphous cloud that engulfs him, and his mind jumps from one catastrophic and negative thought to another, with certain themes quickly taking on epic proportions. He is not thinking about how to book his car in at the service station, but dwelling bitterly on deep psychological fears of poverty and the feelings of failure and humiliation that brings, of his relationship with his father, of how he feels like he's on a rat wheel and the rat wheel is always just about to break . . .

This "head storm" is simply his brain in overdrive. It's normal to look for patterns, elaborate on themes, make predictions, come to conclusions, or ask *why*. But a distressed brain can do this in an out-of-control fashion, becoming completely untethered from reality. How do you tether it back again? By finding and anchoring to the concrete world.

Ask yourself: what can you **do**? Don't imagine the next three weeks or the next ten steps. Just think of the very next concrete action you could take. Chris takes a deep breath and answers this question: He needs to get his car examined at a garage so he knows what the problem is and can get some quotes for repairs. Next step, then, is to make some calls. That's all. It's not his job to think about the *outcome*—just about the next step in the *process*.

Make a detailed and dispassionate list. Acknowledge your emotions as they come up, but politely ask them to sit aside for the moment while you tackle the issue at hand with calm, neutral objectivity. **When you catch your mind wandering, grab a hold of the thought and ask plainly: "Can I do anything about this?"** If the answer is yes, stop ruminating and do that thing. If the answer is no, stop ruminating—since ruminating won't help. Either way, you don't need to ruminate!

When Chris catches the thought, "This morning is just a disaster," he stops and asks if that thought is actionable. Nope. It has no shape. It's just a vaguely threatening cloud that doesn't go anywhere. When the thought, *You just never get a chance to get ahead in this life* crosses his mind, he definitely ignores it. Following it will lead him nowhere.

When he thinks, "I bet fixing that damn car will cost me a fortune," he pauses, then decides to turn it into a question. *Will* it cost him a fortune? He doesn't actually know. He makes a list of three service garages to call and commits to getting a quote from each of them. If it really will cost him a fortune, well, at least he knows this for sure now and can make his next move. In the event the quotes are actually very low, though, he has spared himself a huge amount of useless anxiety.

In fact, as Chris goes about dealing with his morning from hell, he realizes that this is precisely the quality he most admired in his dad—the ability to just get on and do what needs to be done without too much whining, angst, or handwringing. He takes a moment to experience what this new perspective actually feels like. How the problem is still there, but somehow *he* is different in relation to that problem. Chris calls three places, and they agree to send him quotes within the hour. But he discovers that even though nothing much has changed for his situation, he feels much better simply for having taken a positive, proactive step.

If your negative thinking is running out of control, immediately ask it to focus on one *small, concrete detail* right here in the *present*. Forget about grand narratives that will only lead to the distortion of overgeneralization. **One amazing way to get distance and shift perspectives, then, is to get out of your own head and into the concrete, physical world of action.** Sometimes, nothing can dissolve useless rumination, negative thoughts, and pessimism as quickly!

A Word on the Most Useless Habit in the World
When a captive parrot is extremely stressed or unhappy, it can sometimes start to pull its own feathers out. To the dismay of its owner, it will sit and yank out its own feathers one by one so that it has raw, bald patches all over its neck and chest, and a dirty cage filling up with feathers and down. Granted, parrots do this for a range of complicated reasons, but human beings have a tendency to do something similar—a kind of mental feather plucking.

The habit in question is **complaining**. Every time you complain, it is as useless and destructive as a parrot plucking one of their own beautiful, healthy feathers and throwing it to the ground. It serves no purpose, it solves no problem, and all it achieves is to make the parrot look awful. Most of us think of complaining as relatively harmless, but the ease with which we can make little complaints here and there is precisely what makes the problem so insidious.

Consider Christina, another one of Chris's hypothetical colleagues at work. Nothing in particular happens to her that Monday morning, but that doesn't stop her from releasing a steady stream of background complaints throughout the day.

"Ugh! They're out of decaf again. This place is a joke."

"I think I have a headache coming on."

"Have you seen the price of gas lately!?"

"I wish it were Friday."

"So we got the decorators in, but *of course* they messed it up, and now we have to get someone in to fix their work..."

"I'm so tired."

"Gah! This thing's broken again. I just can't handle it."

"That woman at the café was so rude, seriously. Would it have killed her to smile?"

And on and on and on...

Any single one of the above statements might not seem like much on their own, but when *every* sentiment seems to be a mild complaint, the effect is a little like a bald spot on a parrot. Christina isn't having the crisis Chris is, but she is just as surely creating a negative world for herself with her thought patterns.

Complaining is powerful. It is the opposite of gratitude. It is also incompatible with conscious, inspired action.

Complaining is identifying a problem without seeking a solution, or passively whining so that others will solve it for you. It's a subtle way to deny our own responsibility for an issue, or to quietly place blame. It is one hundred percent "out of power" language and can lead to a creeping attitude of victimization.

When we complain, we amplify negativity while doing nothing to actually address it. At its worst, complainers make a nuisance of themselves, and their dissatisfaction can almost be weaponized against others, as though they were constantly saying, "Wah! I'm unhappy, and I'm going to make things unpleasant until someone does something about it!" Basically, complaining is like a low-level, background temper tantrum!

If you recognize a little of yourself in Christina, don't worry—we all complain sometimes. There is nothing wrong with being irritated, tired, sad, or confused. **What matters is what we consciously choose to do about it**. Ask yourself the same question Chris does. Can I do anything about this? Complaining, like pessimism, is a kind of coping mechanism (but a rotten one!). You may discover that it's actually far easier to cope when you remind yourself of a simple fact: If you don't like something, you have the power to change it.

How Is Your Media Hygiene?

Before we move on, let's briefly consider another equally useless habit that may have snuck into your life without you realizing the damage it causes day to day. Remember Christina's list of complaints above? Take a look at the following:

Four-year-old's savage murder "the worst thing I've seen in my life," says commissioner.

Russia destroys Ukrainian hospitals in missile attack.

Weather experts now predict even more extreme weather events for 2024.

Germany's Greens in freefall amid corruption allegations.

The housing crisis is breaking people's brains.

Everything's terrible; slit wrists now.

Okay, so maybe that last one is made up, but you get the idea. If complaining is identifying a problem without also identifying a solution—even just a potential solution—then the doom and gloom that floods into our nervous systems from the media is like turbocharged complaining. It's obvious why: Most of us can do very, very little about the awful things we read about in the news or on social media.

That means that when you mindlessly and endlessly "doomscroll" on your phone, while taking no action, you are essentially amplifying all those bad feelings, while at the same time making yourself feel more and more hopeless (by the way, two key signs of depression—hopelessness and helplessness—are a natural result of exposing yourself to certain kinds of media. It's not a mistake that it makes you feel so apathetic; it's by design).

You don't have to live in a cave or pretend that there aren't problems in the world. But like Chris and Christina, it's worth remembering that you do have the power (perhaps it's even a responsibility) to maintain a certain distance from especially negative material out there in the world. Become mindful of the kind of content you consume.

What effect does it have on your emotions?

What kind of beliefs and thoughts do they encourage?

How do you behave when you think and feel the way you do after taking in such content?

Most of us understand the need to maintain physical hygiene, to protect ourselves from toxins and germs, to avoid UV rays, and to run away from people wielding knives in dark alleys . And yet, we may deliberately choose to waste hours of every day soaking up content in the media that terrifies, saddens, angers, or alienates us. In other words, we have poor media hygiene. The environment can support or hinder us; it can impact the way we feel and the beliefs we hold. If you don't like the way that your media intake is making you think or feel, then you know the solution: Create distance!

Try a Cognitive Defusion Exercise
In reading the stories above about people like Chris or Dan, you can be forgiven for thinking that when it comes to your own life, things are seldom so simple or clear cut. It can often seem like all these ideas make sense . . . but only long after you've already gotten trapped in negative thinking or even had a full-blown episode or panic attack. Whatever term we use to describe this phenomenon when it happens, we have to acknowledge that sometimes, our negative

thoughts get the upper hand on us, and we feel ourselves sinking.

The advantage Dan has is that he can use the ABC framework at his own pace, over many weeks and months with a therapist he trusts. When Chris wakes up to a hellishly bad day, he can gain a little distance and, if he gains control over the negativity spiral, feel better the next day. **But what about when you're *right in the middle of some very negative thoughts and you can't get out?*** One obvious characteristic of really negative thinking is that it warps our ability to see everything, including the problem as it's unfolding. We stop being able to imagine a way out, and start to think that things have always been this bad and will continue to be forever.

Action Commitment Therapy (ACT) is a psychological approach that has a word for this exact feeling of being flooded with negativity: **fusion**.

When we are fused with thoughts, we are so close to them that we cannot think, feel, or act outside of them. The thought consumes us. It *is* us. It's a little like watching a movie and being so engrossed in the unfolding story that you forget you are watching a movie at all (and incidentally, that you can always just walk out!).

In the same way, when we are fused, we forget that we are having thoughts at all. And so we are at their mercy, assuming that our current and transient experience of reality is permanent, unalterable, and completely out of our control.

When we discussed Dan and how distance and perspective gave him enough breathing room to gently challenge and replace his negative thoughts, we were also talking about fusion. However, when we are *really* fused with negative thoughts and ideas, it can often take a lot more than a day or a few perspective shifts to help us change gear.

Your brain is not a machine that perfectly regards reality, but a machine that creates a picture *of* reality, or a story *about* reality. When we are fused with negative thoughts, however, we have told ourselves such a convincing story that we believe it fully and cannot escape.

Ellen's Story and Finding the "Big You"

Ellen's world is a dark, dark place. She has felt broadly miserable about life and herself for as long as she can remember. From the outside, Ellen looks like an ordinary person, and she has friends and family who love her. On the inside, though, Ellen's mind is like a tailor-made torture chamber designed just for her. She doesn't just feel and believe that she is worthless and that life is completely not worth living; she *knows* it's the case.

It is, in fact, the only thing she is ever really sure about. She has gone to therapists of all kinds, tried medication, spoken to friends, read the self-help books, and even once or twice gone to retreats and workshops. But nothing really shifts Ellen's deep, lasting conviction that life is misery, and that to be alive is basically to suffer. Constantly. Yes, she is what people call "depressed." If Ellen's life was a movie, it would be a gritty and miserable black-and-white drama that ends with everyone dying in the apocalypse.

Ellen's thoughts and feelings have been stuck in this mode for so long that they have cemented themselves into core beliefs that form the very foundation on which the rest of her world is built. No matter what happens, Ellen's mental filter makes sure that the only conclusion she can ever reach is, "Life is awful." And Ellen is completely, one hundred percent *fused to this thought*. They are stuck together like glue.

So, when she sits in the therapist's chair, she doesn't ask for coping strategies or help understanding why she can't stop being so negative. Instead, she asks, "Why is life so miserable?"

When she confides in a close friend who is trying to understand how to help her, Ellen can only say, "How can you help me? There's nothing you can do. There's nothing anyone can do—that's why I'm so unhappy in the first place."

When her husband tells her that's she's beautiful and that he loves her, all she can say is, "Well, it must be nice to be so delusional!"

You can see the problem. Not only is Ellen wearing some very black-tinted glasses, she is **completely unaware that she is**. So even when she attempts to solve the problem, she is solving the wrong one. Her position goes deeper than Chris's or Dan's because not only is she at the mercy of some very powerful negative thoughts, she isn't even able to recognize that this (and not the state of the world around her) is the source of her misery.

How on earth does someone like Ellen escape her dark thoughts—in other words, how does she defuse?

Again, it's a question of a mindset shift, i.e., learning to look at the problem on a completely different level. Earlier, we mentioned one way to gain distance from the inner critic: giving it a name and treating it as though it literally was someone separate from you and someone you could send away (remember Mildred?).

Here, we will try to imagine that the Mind (capital M!) in its entirety is a separate entity. This means that you can step back from it and look at it from afar. This poses the question, what is doing the looking? Aren't you your mind? The answer is a resounding NO!

Not only is it a good idea to imagine that your Mind is something separate from you and that you can watch, it's a good idea to connect to that You (capital Y!) that is doing the watching.

"There goes boring old Mildred again, my old friend the inner critic, coming up with a million reasons to tell **me** why I can't do something. Get out of here, Mildred!"

The me in the above statement is You—the big You.

This may seem like a weird philosophical point to labor, but it's important because by doing this (separating your Mind from You), you are giving yourself a powerful **lever** to get out of any trap that your Mind puts you in.

Let's imagine how this might work for Ellen. Let's say she's having an especially dark time and is feeling completely overwhelmed by the negativity she sees around her in the world. All she can see is that the world is a dark, chaotic place filled with greedy, crazy people who seem hellbent on hurting one another (you've probably had a similar thought at some point or other, right?). Her brain is like a hurricane of negativity, so she sits down with a journal to try to release some of it onto the page.

She writes,

I just don't see the point of it all. I work so hard, and it's basically for nothing. Why bother trying? I could go out there and start a new project and get all hopeful and blah blah blah, but someone will only come and smash it all down. That's not to say I'd even get to finish anything in the first place, because I'm too tired. How many things have I started and never finished? I don't have the time, and honestly, there isn't really a thing I'm good at—not in this world. Maybe if I were a cut-throat psychopath or something, but I'm not. So I just don't care anymore.

Phew! A negativity hurricane, indeed. But let's look closer. On the advice of her therapist, Ellen tries something different. She puts everything down on paper, then looks at the notebook. She takes her pen and draws a big box around all the words. In a different-color pen, she writes above it in bigger letters: THIS IS WHAT MY MIND IS TELLING ME. Because Ellen's quite creative, she cleverly turns the box into a speech bubble, which is coming from the mouth of a little grumpy face in the corner of the page.

And just like that, there are *two* voices. Ellen's and this little grumpy face on the page. Now, Ellen might do this exercise and *still* side with the negative thoughts. The difference is that this time, she's done so knowing that this point of view is *not* the only game in town. She is aware now that she has chosen it; in other words, she starts to see her negative perspective not as reality, but as a negative perspective.

Ellen does this for a few days, and after a while, a lightbulb goes off: She looks at all the negativity on the page (that's outside her head and somewhere out there where she can see it) and thinks, "Wow. *That's* what I carry in my head all the time. That's messed up."

Does Ellen cure herself overnight of her negative thinking? No. It took her a lifetime to learn. But the next time she has one of her darker days and she sits with her journal again, she notices all those same thoughts again, just as before. Except now, she's not quite so tied to them. She watches herself have them. The change is subtle, but after some time, something happens. She thinks to herself one day, *I'm feeling depressed* instead of *life sucks*.

The great thing about a lever is that it can work to shift an enormous load even if you can only fit the narrow end of the wedge in at first. Once Ellen gets the smallest inkling **she is not her thoughts, she is just having thoughts**, that realization grows and grows. One day, Ellen picks up her journal again and flips through pages and pages of negative thoughts she has put down over the weeks and months. She asks herself a question: Is this really what I want? She is no longer wondering why life is so bad for her; she is wondering whether the thought that life is bad is actually helping her in any way.

The end of this story is not that Ellen permanently vanquishes depression from her life forever—it hardly ever works out that way. But she does something far more impressive, if you think about it. *Ellen learns to think outside of her own mind.* She starts to look at the thoughts in her head not as absolute truth but as arbitrary tools—some of them are useful, some aren't. Some build her up and give her courage and fill her life with meaning, and some make her feel despairing and trapped. Some are rational and some aren't. Some inspire action, and others convince you that action is even possible.

For those who battle with depression, the biggest trap is to think, "I'm unhappy because life is so unbearable," but it really might be the other way around: because you are fused with the thought that life is unbearable, you feel unhappy as a consequence.

Make Your Beliefs Earn Their Keep

A thought is just a thought.

It's not automatically the "truth."

You don't have to act on it.

You don't have to agree with it.

You don't have to respond to it at all.

It doesn't have to *mean* anything about the situation at hand, or you as a person.

It's not good or bad.

It's just a thought.

Once you realize a thought is just a thought, then you are able to let it do what thoughts do best: pass. Here is a question: If a bus suddenly pulled up in front of you right now, would you automatically board it and allow it to take you away? Well, you'd probably want to know where it was going first. That's how you should think about thoughts.

Where does this thought take me? Do I want to go there?

If not, don't board the bus. Let it go on its way and don't attach to it or fuse with it. It's not your bus. It has nothing to do with you. If it *does* take you where you want to go, then get on board—and forget about all the other buses. In fact, get behind the wheel and steer that bus yourself to the destination of your choice. Stay on the bus as long as it helps you get where you need to go, and when it doesn't, find another vehicle or another route there. The bus system is there, after all, to serve *you*. It's there to help you navigate your city and get around. Thoughts are the same. They're there for you. And not everything that pops into your head deserves your full attention and buy-in. In fact, the vast majority of them don't!

This turns the relationship between You and your Mind on its head. Instead of your Mind calling the shots. You are the one in charge. You make your thoughts earn their keep. Unless they are accurate, productive, supportive, congruent with your values, practically useful, or, at the very least, pleasant, then you have no use for them. So you can let them go.

Ellen did this when she looked at the steaming pile of negativity she was holding on to and realized it did precisely *nothing* for her. It wasn't on her side. It wasn't helping. You don't have to be in as bad a state of Ellen, though, to do the same. Try the following:

1. Ask yourself what you value most in life, or what you are trying to achieve. Maybe it's something big like the love of your family, personal growth, or your faith. Maybe at the moment, all you can think of is something immediate like "some peace and quiet" or "a less crummy job." Even in the most negative mindsets, we all want *something*. Hold that thought in your mind.
2. Now, like Ellen did, become aware of the negative thoughts that are coming up for you.
3. Take a close look at this thought. Tell yourself, "I am having this thought." Pause and let it sink in that this is your Mind talking, and it's just a thought. If you like, give it another label, too. Call it by its name: criticism, doubt, curiosity, fear, observation, resistance, etc. Get acquainted with what kind of thought it is. Create some distance by using third person, if you like, "Ellen is having a self-hating thought."

4. Now, don't worry about whether the thought is "true" or not; instead, ask if it matches up with what you identified in Step 1 as something you want or value. **Is this thought going to take you closer to or further away from that thing?**
5. If the thought takes you closer, then great. If it doesn't, or if it's neutral, you now have a *choice*. Will you actively choose something that goes against what you already know you want? Or will you let it pass by? You also get to choose whether you'd like to spend your time and your brainpower on a thought that *will* help you get what you want. (Yes! Thoughts can be your servants and work for you!)
6. Do this as often as you like. Thoughts are a bit like buses—there's always another one on its way...

Ellen does it like this:

Though she's not happy about much in her life, she does love her husband, and she does care about her pets and her nieces and nephews. Even in her negative state of mind, she can identify that she wants her husband to be happy, and that she wants to spend time with her nieces and nephews and be a responsible pet owner.

One Saturday morning, she's lounging in bed and feeling despondent. The thought pops into her mind: "You're a waste of space, slobbing around in bed all day while other people are living their lives!" She immediately stops this thought in its tracks and examines it. She even says aloud to herself, "Hello, Depression, I see that you're speaking right now." She realizes she's having a negative thought. Now, in this precious empty space after this realization, she understands that she has a choice. She can decide what to do next.

She thinks about her husband, her nieces and nephews, her dogs. Does thinking that she's a waste of space make her a better wife? Does it help her get closer to her nieces and nephews? Does it help her take care of her pets? No. At best, it does nothing; at worst, it gets in the way. If she gets on that bus, she will soon start thinking other thoughts, too. That she is worthless, that she may as well not be here, and so on. In that moment, even though she still feels despondent, she decides to let the thought go. She can't cancel it out or pretend she didn't have it. But she decides she won't *continue* to have it. In a few minutes, she experiments with changing the thought. She could say, "How lucky am I to have a nice cozy moment in bed on such a peaceful Saturday morning?" She notices how it feels to hold on to this thought, instead.

It's Never a War

You'll notice that Ellen doesn't kick the negative thought to the curb and yell at it. She doesn't go head to head and wrestle it into submission. She just *doesn't* hold on to it. That's a big difference.

Before we conclude this chapter, it's worth mentioning how defusion is not about fighting off a negative thought. That's because resisting a negative thought is just another way to fuse with it. If we are fearfully or angrily resisting a thought, we are just as much at its mercy as if we were closely identifying with it.

When you become aware of a thought, just keep it at that level—awareness. Try avoid taking the extra step of adding on your own judgment or interpretation of that thought. Try not to criticize a thought, condemn yourself for having it, or even be pleased because it's a "good" thought. Just be aware. You *will* appraise the thought, but only in terms of its usefulness, i.e., whether it really serves any purpose in your life.

If you do notice that judgment, resistance, or clinging coming up, that's fine too. It's just one more thing to notice! Maybe you think, "I could kill him," but instantly think, "You shouldn't be so angry." There's no point judging the second thought, either, and feeling bad because you felt bad about feeling bad! Just stop, ask what is working and what isn't, and let the thoughts go. Remind yourself that thoughts can't hurt you or anyone. They only mean something when you decide they do.

Psychiatrist and much-loved author of the inspirational book *Man's Search for Meaning*, Viktor Frankl, once said, "Between stimulus and response there is a space, and in that space lies our growth and our freedom." You don't have to have everything figured out, or magically turn your thought process around until you're thinking the "right" way. If all you can manage is to pause and realize that you are thinking in the first place, then you have already done so much. Hold on to that pause.

Remind yourself of your conscious choice. You don't even have to make a decision yet; just be aware it's there. You might find that you actually like not having to respond or choose . . . isn't it nice to just let negative thoughts do what they want and burn themselves out and dissipate all on their own, without you having to get worked up about them in the least?

Summary

- To rewrite our negative thought patterns, we "can't solve problems by using the same kind of thinking we used when we created them."

- We can use the ABCDE acronym (activating event, belief, consequence, disputation, and new event) and explore the stories we're telling in a thought journal. We can decide whether a new alternative is a good one according to its accuracy, helpfulness, and congruence with our values.
- Once you've identified your current thoughts, ask if there's a different way to think about things, and how you can bring that idea to life with concrete action. Seek out evidence for a new belief, practice self-compassion, and go into learning mode, asking questions instead of making statements.
- Negativity can be relieved by shifting perspectives and creating psychological distance. Remember that pessimism, negativity, and gloomy nihilism are all coping mechanisms and once served a purpose. But right now, we can choose to cope with adversity in different, healthier ways (and there always will be adversity!)
- Create spatial, temporal, and psychological distance from distressing thoughts, ask what others might do in our situation (role-switching), and turn your mind to concrete action instead of asking why. Focus on a small, concrete detail in the present and ask what you can **do**. Avoid identifying problems without seeking solutions—i.e., complaining! Be mindful of your media use

and minimize negative content that is draining you.
- When we are stuck in intense emotions, we can try the ACT technique of defusion. Imagine that your Mind is something separate from you and that you can watch it.
- Remember that you are not your thoughts; you are just having thoughts. Make your thoughts earn their keep!

Chapter 3: Master the Art of Distress Tolerance and Self-Soothing

Perhaps you read about Ellen's tales of woe and thought, "Fair enough . . . but some of us have *real* problems we're dealing with." This is a good observation—sometimes, people think negatively... because they're simply responding to something negative in their environment.

Few of us will get through life without experiencing an emotional crisis, a big loss, an upheaval, or an accident at some point or another. It's one thing to learn to master your thought processes so that you're not creating unnecessary suffering for yourself—but it's another when you're faced with a legitimately negative circumstance that cannot be avoided. What then?

In this chapter, we'll talk about distress tolerance and how to cultivate it. This is a set of skills that most people don't really think about until they're in a crisis situation and need them urgently. But many of the same principles of defusing, perspective-switching, reframing, and challenging your cognitive distortions can be used when we're facing a situation that makes us feel out of control. Call it a toolkit of crisis survival skills!

The tools we'll describe below can be used when

- you're in extreme pain—emotionally or physically,
- there's a formidable temptation that you have to resist,
- you're dealing with a temporary but very challenging situation that can't be avoided,
- it's an emergency and you have to be productive and focused . . . even though you're completely overwhelmed,
- there's a conflict and you need to put aside raw emotions to communicate effectively,
- you're absolutely terrified but need to act wisely anyway.

A crisis can put a major dent in anyone's sense of emotional mastery and control. **When the**

chips are down, it's easy to slip back into old patterns of behavior or default to clumsy, destructive, or unconscious ways of coping. Trouble is, though these habits may feel momentarily soothing, they ultimately create more problems and set up negative feedback loops that keep amplifying themselves.

Alex has hurt his back at his job. He's received some worker's comp, but he's basically off duty until he gets better. He's at home alone (his partner works all day), the doctors and physiotherapists don't feel like they're helping, and there's no end in sight. His boss has been kind enough, but Alex knows it's only a matter of time before they need to let him go. His back is getting worse, not better, and Alex is unsure how they'll fund the enormously expensive surgery if he needs it, or what they'll do for money once his savings and insurance money are gone.

In other words, Alex is in a crisis. He's in pain and can't be prescribed any more painkillers since they're addictive. But on some days, the pain is so intense, Alex doesn't know what to do with himself. He can't move. He's depressed, anxious, bored, lonely, scared, and exhausted. And every day, he faces excruciating pain that doesn't let up. What can he do?

Alex's "solution" is threefold: He soothes himself with comfort eating and junk food, he sits immobile on the sofa for hours-long marathon gaming sessions, and he starts abusing alcohol. These things don't help exactly, but they make everything a little more bearable. They also make everything worse. Within a few months, Alex is not only depressed, anxious, bored, lonely, scared, and exhausted, he's also gaining weight, usually drunk or hungover, and staying up until 3 a.m. every night and sleeping past noon the next day.

Nobody would say that Alex doesn't have a legitimate "reason" to feel negative. Nobody could say that he is to blame, and most would agree that the way he is dealing with the crisis is understandable, even if not ideal. However, the irony is that Alex's methods for dealing with distress have become their own form of distress. Alex cannot help that he injured his back; however, he doesn't have the skills needed to survive the crisis, and in a way, this is a bigger problem.

The coping mechanisms he's chosen are **false coping mechanisms** because, ultimately, they create more of the problem, exacerbate suffering, and keep him trapped where he is. The more he drinks, the less emotionally available he is for his partner, and the worse they communicate. This means that the coping mechanism of drinking robs him of an important source of potential support: a loving relationship.

The more junk food he eats, the worse his overall health. This means that "comfort" eating is actually impeding his body's ability to heal quickly. The extra pounds that make it even more difficult to complete the exercises the physiotherapist prescribed make him feel anything but "comfort"! The late-night gaming is just as addictive. It's a welcome distraction, but it also makes him angry and combative, and since he's ruined his natural sleep cycles, his anxiety and depression get worse, not better.

In a crisis, the challenge of staying calm, positive, rational, and accepting may seem like a Herculean task. It may seem almost impossible. Let's be honest, it's not something you *want* to do. But the point of Alex's story is to show that living the life that false coping mechanisms create is actually much, much harder! We don't tolerate distress because we enjoy it and have to learn to grin and bear it. We tolerate distress because it is *less hard work and less suffering* than allowing ourselves to be swallowed by it.

How to Self-Soothe
In life, pain is inevitable. But we have a choice in how we respond to it.

Self-soothing is a way to acknowledge and accept pain that is inevitable—*without making it any bigger than it should be*.

When you rail against pain and loss and injustice, you are actually prolonging and expanding that negativity. You are placing all of your focused attention on that pain and amplifying it. There's nothing wrong with this response—in fact, your ancient ancestors evolved this hyper-focus on pain because it forced them to go into problem-solving mode and quickly remove or escape from the threat in order to survive.

If someone has done something to hurt you, one way to cope could be to hyperfocus on their guilt and get caught in a loop blaming them again and again. This feels good . . . for a short while, at least. It's good to use the opportunity to adjust your boundaries, change your process, reassess a relationship, or just forgive and move on. Once you've genuinely done this, though, there is no reason to keep dwelling on the fact of the other person's guilt (i.e., hold a grudge) since that's really just a way of telling yourself over and over, "I'm powerless. I'm hurt. It's not fair . . ." Not unlike pressing on a bruise so it can't heal properly!

But there are some types of pain that *cannot* be escaped. For these types of pain, struggling and resisting can only *add* to the portion of pain you have to suffer through. The person who complains that it is raining has one additional problem compared to the person who knows it is but chooses to just carry on with life instead of focusing on the fact.

Self-soothing is not the same as distraction or avoidance or having a little rant about how unfair life is. Rather, it's about being kind enough to yourself that you refuse to add any more to the suffering you're experiencing, whether it's a suffering on the scale Alex is experiencing or something more trivial like a rainy day. If you genuinely cannot do anything to remove a pain (and we will look in a later chapter at an excellent way to figure this out for yourself), then the only rational next step is to do what you can to bear it.

<u>Grounding</u> is a great way to self-soothe. When you anchor into your senses, you are pulling your conscious mind away from anxieties, ruminations, regrets, and fears that are based in the past and present, and asking it to rest gently in the present instead. The irony is that we create a lot of drama for ourselves trying to run away from a painful moment in the present we think is too much to handle. But if we did stay

with it for a while, we'd see that it wasn't as bad as we thought it was.

Your five senses are your gateway to the present. Pause, breathe, and become aware. Take five minutes to find something to dwell on for each sense—without judgment or any agenda at all. For Alex, when his back pain reaches distracting levels, instead of defaulting to addictive behaviors, he pauses, takes a deep breath, and makes a conscious choice *not to run away*.

He looks closely at the texture of the sofa cushion and the almost infinite shades of blue he can discern in the weave of the fabric. He listens to the faint buzz of the refrigerator in the next room that he hadn't noticed before. He smells the reassuring and faint aroma of laundry softener in the blanket on his lap. He touches the blanket; there are places where his own rough skin catches against it. He can sense the lingering taste of coffee still on his tongue from his morning cup . . .

After a few minutes, Alex isn't magically not in pain anymore. But, what seemed completely overwhelming and engulfing a moment before doesn't seem so big anymore. He has done something different—instead of fleeing pain, he has anchored into the present and ridden it out.

TIPP Skills

Anyone can see that Alex isn't helping himself by eating garbage, being sedentary, and wasting hours staring at screens. It's obvious that maltreating the physical body this way can only cause psychological, social, cognitive, emotional, and even spiritual damage. But we seldom appreciate the fact that this relationship goes the other way, too: If we soothe and regulate the physical body first, we can calm down the central nervous system and improve our psychological state.

TIPP stands for

Temperature
Intense Exercise
Paced Breathing
Paired Muscle Relaxation

These four things can immediately calm down an aggravated limbic system and lower your overall arousal. Physical arousal influences and informs psychological arousal.

Try cold water. Splashing the face with cool water actually activates what is called the "mammalian dive response," which is an ancient adaptation that results in slower heart rate, slower breath rate, and an overall calmed nervous system. Have a quick, cold shower, rub an ice cube on your neck or wrists, or dip your feet in cool lake or seawater, if you can. Cold temperatures affect your body's metabolism, limbic system, and homeostatic balance, with the overall effect of making you feel calmer. Even fanning your face to create a little cooling breeze can help you, quite literally, cool off.

Get moving. Intense exercise likewise has a balancing and regulating effect on the body. A burst of intense physical activity releases adrenaline and creates momentary euphoria. Hard exercise is a healthy distraction that floods your body with oxygenated blood, and the increased heart rate reinvigorates every tissue and organ of the body. Do anything that gets you panting for air, makes you sweat, or brings some color to your cheeks! Nothing helps a tangled up, distressed mind as much as taking inspired action. And what could be more active than . . . well, being active?

If you don't feel like a jog, do something else to get your heart rate up. Get stuck into decluttering and deep cleaning your house, chop wood, play with a child, dance, or even punch a pillow if you're feeling angry or overwhelmed. All of it counts, so long as you are getting back into your breathing, moving body, and out of your head (it goes without saying that this step needs to be adapted if the pain you're trying to tolerate is purely physical. Even if you're hurt or ill, however, you'll feel better and more in control if you breathe deeply, stretch, and gently push yourself to your physical limit, whatever it happens to be).

Pace your breathing. Your breathing and your emotional state are closely connected. If you are breathing slowly, deeply, and rhythmically, you simply cannot be in a panicked or overwhelmed state. Just try it! Inhale slowly for a count of two or three, pause, then exhale with control for a count of two or three. As you do so, imagine your blood pressure and heart rate dropping.

Remind yourself that as you breathe, you feel. If your breathing is shallow and constricted, then your emotions will be similarly tight and tense. If your breathing is irregular, so, too, will your thoughts be. Remember that the relationship goes both ways—how you breathe impacts how you feel, but how you feel impacts how you breathe. Changing either one will change the other.

Use PMR—paired muscle relaxation. Choose a pair of muscles (for example, the tops of both thighs or the muscles in each big toe) and tighten them as hard as you can as you inhale. Hold it, then very slowly and with control release the tension as you exhale. It is difficult to be emotionally tense and agitated if your muscles are relaxed.

Tensing muscles before relaxing leads to a deeper calm. Repeat a few times and then move on to another paired muscle till you have worked through your entire body. This is an excellent mind-body connector that allows you to slow down, go quiet, and release. It can be paired with paced breathing and is especially useful in bed at night to help you get to sleep.

You don't have to run through your entire body if you don't have time, however. Just choose a muscle, focus, breathe deeply, and ground yourself in the sensation. Try to imagine that your brain can only ever be in one of two places—out there in the past or the future or in no man's land, thinking up hypotheticals, or it can be in the here and now. If you bring it firmly into the here and now (where your body is), you automatically pull it away from anxious or unhelpful thoughts. You get closer to your real, lived, embodied experience, while creating that magical distance between you and your thoughts.

There is one huge advantage to using TIPP: your mind is not required! You can notice negative thoughts, temptations, upset emotions, and anxious loops. Yet you don't have to deal with them at all, but engage on the level of your body alone. So many of the more psychological self-soothing techniques don't work because they're attempted with a body that is aroused. If you try to have a rational argument with yourself about why you shouldn't panic, for example, it won't really sink in if your heart is racing, your muscles are tense, and your blood pressure is through the roof. You need to relax first and *then* engage at the level of thoughts, feelings, and rational arguments.

The TIPP technique is excellent for creating calm in the immediate moment. Once you lower your overall limbic system arousal, you likely can start to think more clearly, and deliberately choose more helpful coping mechanisms. For the longer term, keep thinking of your body and how if you support it, it will support you:

- Eat well. Cut out processed foods and make plants and quality protein the backbone of every meal. Avoid the physiological stress of fasting, and give yourself nice, smooth blood sugar levels by eating small balanced meals more regularly.
- Avoid dehydration by drinking plenty of water and tea throughout the day.
- Maintain a regular sleep pattern—the number of hours is not as important as the consistency of the routine. Keep the same sleep and wake times every day.
- Stay away from stimulants—that includes coffee and sugar. You don't have to abstain, just be mindful and keep an

eye on staying balanced and even, rather than chasing extremes.
- Try yoga or other deep stretching techniques. You'll regulate your breathing, strengthen the mind-body connection, get your blood and lymph system flowing, oxygenate your tissues, and keep supple.

For Alex, his situation improves when he starts incorporating a specific habit into his routine. Though he can't stand for long periods, he does a morning workout where he uses his arms and adapts exercises so he can do them lying down. Once he is hot and sweaty, he cools off in a cold shower and finishes off with a brisk rub with a towel. He finds that no matter how much of a bad mood he started with, he always feels a little more alive and in control when he starts mornings this way.

He is also learning that when the physical pain gets too intense, he can distract himself by grounding and using breathing exercises. He is also finding that paired muscle relaxation at night before bed helps stop a racing mind and lets him get better quality sleep. These things are not miraculous, but they allow Alex to lower his arousal levels so that he is more receptive to other strategies like the above—thought restructuring, reframing, and so on. The pain is still there, and the problem is still a problem, but his response to it is now adaptive and masterful.

What Radical Acceptance Really Means

Most of us have an incorrect understanding of what the word "acceptance" means. We resist accepting things that feel bad because we think that it means we agree with them, that we want them to continue, or that we are passively condoning what we know is wrong. We think that if we accept something, it means we are somehow making it more likely that it will keep continuing. If somebody walks up to us in the street and tries to hand us their bag of trash, then of course we don't have to "accept" it.

But radical acceptance is not about accepting in the ordinary sense of the word. For some more fundamental aspects of reality, we are *not* being offered the choice or asked, "Do you want this?" We are not asked if we like it or agree with it. In fact, our agreement seems utterly irrelevant to whether we get it or not! Some parts of reality are up for debate, and others aren't. We can choose to live a healthy life and to be safe and avoid catching germs. But we cannot choose whether or not we die. We can choose how we respond to crises and emergencies, but not whether those events happen in the first place. For the parts of reality that are not up for debate, we need **radical acceptance, which is basically the decision to stop fighting reality**.

When we take action against something we don't like but can change, then we have a chance of changing it.

When we take action against something we don't like but *cannot* change, it stays exactly as it is, and we only become bitter, resentful, or exhausted.

You can accept reality without liking it. You can accept reality without liking it and still live a meaningful life. You can make choices and take action on some things even if you don't get to decide on others. Life can be hard but manageable.

In fact, acceptance can sometimes be the one thing that makes a bad situation pass more quickly. Imagine a woman in labor. At the first sensations of pain, she is terrified and thinks, "I can't do this. I don't want to do this. I hate this." What happens is that, because her mind is completely unaccepting, her body follows suit and tenses up completely, trying to push back against that pain.

But because she is tense and resistant, the labor becomes more difficult. Her muscles don't relax enough, so the process becomes more difficult and more painful. She gets even more terrified, tenses up further, and soon there is a full-blown crisis. Her lack of acceptance has, in effect, prolonged and amplified the pain. If she had instead accepted the pain, she would have relaxed, and the birth would have been easier. What happens physiologically during birth can also be said to happen psychologically and mentally whenever we encounter something we think we don't want, don't like, can't accept. The irony is that when we fight pain, it is often *extra* painful, and we only set ourselves up to get the exact opposite of what we want.

Easier said than done, of course! Let's imagine that Alex is making strides, but after a few months, the doctors tell him they will need to operate. They also tell him that the procedure carries a roughly fifteen percent chance of resulting in total paralysis from the waist down. Ouch. This fact is like a brick wall he smashes into. Alex researches, gets second opinions, and gathers what data he can, but in the end, he still faces an immovable fact: He needs an operation that has a moderate risk of permanently paralyzing him. If he doesn't operate, his life will become unbearable and he may damage his spinal column even further. Alex thinks, "This shouldn't be happening. I can't deal with this. This is not fair. I can't face it."

How can Alex accept this horrible "choice" he has? How could he, heaven forbid, possibly accept being paralyzed, should that be the outcome? You may not be facing a reality quite so stark as Alex's, but the process he uses to find acceptance is exactly the same one you can use when you find yourself "arguing with reality":

Step 1: Acknowledge that you are in fact fighting against reality. Really take a moment to let it sink in that you are pushing against an object that cannot move. Did you notice the word "should" in Alex's thought? Notice your struggle. Notice what it feels like in your body—tension, queasiness, etc.

Step 2: Tell yourself that it cannot be changed. This is harder than it seems. Just like complaining is focusing on a problem without the active effort to change it, wrestling with reality is a negative reaction that does precisely zero to change the facts.

Step 3: Be honest about the reality you face. If you must accept it, know what you're accepting. The truth is always easier to bear when you can see all sides of it! Look at cause and effect. Become curious about the details.

Step 4: Imagine how you would behave if you did accept these facts. What steps would you take (or not take)? How would you cope? What would you choose?

Step 5: Embrace and honor how you feel. Just because you are accepting your reality, it doesn't mean that you suddenly don't feel how you feel. Completely acknowledge any feelings of anger, regret, sadness, or disappointment.

Step 6: Remind yourself of what matters. Life is still worth living even though you are in pain at this moment. Remember the things you value, the principles that guide you, and the dreams you're hoping to achieve. It may be that you have to postpone or re-size these dreams. That's okay. Re-negotiate your future and start to be curious about the meaning you can make from your experience.

The ACCEPTS Skill

This acronym stands for:

A – Activities
C – Contribute
C – Comparisons
E – Emotions, i.e., trying on emotions the opposite to the ones you have
P – Push away or shelve the problem
T – Thoughts, i.e., keeping your mind busy on other tasks and not on crisis-related thoughts and feelings
S – Sensations, i.e., grounding in the five senses as described above

For Alex, this might look like:

A – Stays busy with exercises, hobbies, DIY at home, cooking, and pushing himself to do walks when he can

C – Volunteering with a mental health crisis helpline, which he can do from home and which brings him some satisfaction that he can help others

C – *Helpful* comparisons—he realizes that as bad as his injury is, it could have been worse, and that he was in many ways lucky to have received the support he did

E – When he feels absolute despair, he tries to laugh at himself and have a sense of humor about the situation

P – Overwhelmed at the decision he has to make (operate or don't operate?), he chooses to just rest and process for a while, shelving the decision until he's calmer

T – Keeps his mind busy writing shopping lists, making detailed budgets, solving riddles, or planning for a DIY project in detail

S – Does a grounding exercise every time he can feel his thoughts spiraling into negativity again

As you can see, even in a situation that feels totally hopeless, you always have a choice, and there is a lot you can do even when it feels like there isn't! At the same time, **distress tolerance is a set of skills to help you survive and cope—it is not a long-term strategy for living**

your best life. It's there as a crutch to help you deal with distress without making things worse. But it's not enough on its own. Sooner or later, Alex has to decide whether to get the operation or not.

If you're ever overcome with negative feelings, know that you always have the tools to calm yourself down physically, self-soothe, accept what is happening, and find ways to cope with the most intense emotions as you ride them out. These tools won't solve the problem—but they will help you make it through the worst of it in one piece until you're ready to look at solutions when you're feeling stronger and clearer.

Brain Dumping, Mental Noting, and Scheduled Worry Time

Chris had trouble navigating annoying and irritating life obstacles.

Carrie had to challenge the distorted mental filters she was using to look at herself.

Dan battled to reframe the story of guilt and shame he was living inside.

Ellen struggled to step outside of her depression and low mood.

And Alex had to learn to cope with the very real limitations of physical pain.

Each of these people had to deal with very different problems, but ultimately, each of them worked through their own version of negative thinking and how to find a way out of it. There is one manifestation of negativity that we haven't yet considered, though, and that's anxiety. This chapter is for you if you find your negativity taking the shape of worry, rumination, overthinking, and stress.

In the spirit of radical acceptance and not fighting against our mind or against reality, we'll begin with **a basic CBT principle when dealing with anxiety: We are not attempting to force ourselves not to worry**. It's just like being told "don't think of a pink elephant." Merely saying it makes you think of a pink elephant! So, first things first: getting anxious about your anxiety and worrying about your worry is not going to get you anywhere.

Instead, tap into the capital letter You and remind yourself that you have a choice. In the technique of "worry postponement," we essentially tell ourselves, "Okay, Mind, you have full permission to worry. I'm not stopping you. All I'm going to do is decide *when* you get to do it and for how long." In fact, tell yourself that your intention is to **worry more efficiently**. So, for example, you decide that instead of worrying right this instant, you're going to deliberately worry later tonight at 6 p.m. for twenty minutes.

Scheduling your negativity and worry may seem like an odd thing to do, but it works. This is because

1. You're learning to be aware that you are in fact worrying. (Again, it's about gaining distance—it's not, "Money's tight!" but, "I'm having a stressful thought about money right now.")
2. You avoid getting tangled up in that worry but also avoid going to war with it, resisting it, or denying it.

3. You take control. Just because a thought pops up and says, "Look at me!" it doesn't mean you have to obey.
4. You gain a deeper sense of how worry actually plays out in your life—how it comes and goes, rises and falls, and in time, how utterly useless it usually is . . .
5. You put yourself in a proactive state of mind where you stop worrying and start *strategizing*.

Anxiety is exactly the kind of mental activity that, if not engaged with, will eventually dissipate. You can probably think of a few things you were really worried about a day or a week or ten years ago, and which barely even register with you now. Why? Simply because some time has passed.

When you schedule your worry to take place some other time, you may notice how often you actually forget about it when the allotted worry time rolls around. Or, when the time comes and you have free rein to worry to your heart's content, you realize that the issue just doesn't seem that important anymore. Sometimes, when you arrive at your future worry appointment, you discover that you don't even *want* to worry anymore, that you are feeling way more calm and able to deal with any negativity that remains, or that the negativity has already resolved by itself.

Here's how worry postponement might look in practice.

Be Mindful

You're noticing a recurrent them here, right? It all starts with simply being aware that you are having anxious thoughts and worries in the first place. Just perceive and observe; don't judge. Try not to be too hard on yourself if you notice a worry spiral that seems to be getting out of hand. Try to practice a little radical acceptance.

"I'm feeling extremely worried and anxious at the moment."

"I am feeling so on edge. My stomach's in knots."

"I keep having the thought *what if* and am having trouble stopping it."

Postpone

Even if you have to do it out loud, give yourself permission to worry; only, the worry has to be deferred to a time of your choosing. Make sure that the time you choose is at least a couple hours away (to give your mental state time to change) but not so far off that you unconsciously feel like it won't really happen. Write down

- the day, date, and time,
- the duration for the worry,
- what you will worry about.

For example, let's say you're worrying about an upcoming performance review at work. You notice your anxious overthinking: *"Maybe it'll be really embarrassing. What am I going to do if they keep talking about the incident in March? It may be that they've already discussed it amongst themselves already. Maybe everyone has discussed it, and they're getting ready to fire me at this very moment. What if I cry or get angry during the meeting? What if I say something I regret...?"*

You stop and become mindful and realize that your anxious thoughts are getting carried away. You say out loud, "That's okay, but we're not worrying right now." In a notebook, you scribble down "11 a.m. Tuesday, ten minutes worry time, concerns about upcoming performance review." Then you close the notebook. You've made an agreement with yourself, and so you don't have to keep worrying.

Follow Through

Naturally, your mind will soon start up again with worries. "Do you think you should maybe prepare a few clever rebuttals for if they want to talk about what happened in March? Just in case?" You notice this, and you don't argue with it. You also don't act or respond in any way. "No, Mind, we aren't doing this now—we're worrying tomorrow at 11 a.m., remember?"

Actively remind yourself that the big important issue your brain is trying to draw your attention to will certainly get the attention it deserves . . . in due course. Tell yourself that you're allowed to focus on the present moment's tasks because the worry is actually taken care of for now. All the time from now until 11 a.m. tomorrow is now "free." When the thought pops up, confidently tell it, "Oh, don't worry, I've already dealt with you!"

What about when 11 a.m. comes around? Well, do as you said you would and sit down and worry for ten minutes. But really worry! Don't let your mind wander to *other* worries—just the one you said you'd tackle. You may as well really go for it because once the ten minutes are up, you're not going to think about it anymore. Notice what happens when you do this. You might

1. no longer care about this problem,

2. feel better able to cope with it or manage it,
3. realize an action you can take to fix it,
4. still be at square one with no solution in sight.

Almost always, the outcome will be 1, 2, or 3. Occasionally, though, you will chew over something, and it will still be bothering you. Try your best to ask if there is one small thing you can do, there and then, to improve the situation. Then schedule that in, and promptly forget about it. If you catch yourself worrying further—then repeat the process. Postpone that worry till another time. At the very least, you are limiting your exposure to a difficult situation that you cannot do anything about.

You might start to notice that you keep worrying about something that either a) never comes, or b) does come and isn't as bad as you thought it would be, or even c) it does come, it *is* that bad, and it doesn't matter because you were able to cope with it.

One variation of this practice is to externalize worries while you're postponing them. So whatever pops into your mind, imagine that you're redirecting it to the page and writing it down there. The rule is, once it's written down in the worry book, it does not need to be in your head anymore. The worry book is like a repository. All through the day, collect little nagging fears and concerns as they crop up and put them aside to mull over later, on your own terms.

After a while of doing this, ask yourself a few questions:

Are there any recurrent themes?
How often does the thing you fear actually come to pass?
Is there any difference in outcome when you do worry versus when you don't?

A final variation is called "brain dumping," and it's exactly what it sounds like. When it's your scheduled time to worry, go all out and put EVERYTHING down on the page. You can rant, you can rave, you can say what you like and let it all out. For five whole minutes (try not to go too much longer than this!), you have no limits and can experience the full cathartic power of worrying as hard as you can worry.

Imagine that your brain is like a room in a house that has just become too cluttered with junk. When you do a brain dump, you're basically throwing all this clutter out. The power lies in acknowledging the thoughts and putting them outside of yourself. A big reason we worry is because our brain thinks it's being useful. It wants to keep drawing our attention to something that may be threatening or a problem in the future, but if you put it down on paper, this sends a strong message to your unconscious mind: "I've noted this. It's being dealt with. I won't forget. You can stop reminding me now!"

What should you include in your brain dump? Whatever you need to. Scribble down stream-of-consciousness ideas, thoughts, feelings, and fears. Put down things you're worried about forgetting on your to-do list. Regrets, concerns, complaints—anything you like.

What you do with your brain dump from there is up to you—the wonderful thing is that once it's out on paper, you can do something about it. Here are a few options:

- Burn, crumple, or throw away the paper if what you've expressed is just useless or destructive material. Breathe a sigh of relief.
- Process what you've written. Pick one thing that's bugging you and consciously decide to take a step to address it. Just one thing, though—you can't tackle it all!
- Go through the material, identify negative and self-defeating beliefs, and gently rewrite them. Turn them into affirmations that you begin the following day with. The ABC method described

above can be a great technique to incorporate here.
- If it makes sense to you, pray about or meditate on some of the things that are weighing on your heart but you're stuck with. Ask a higher power to help you carry the burden, or do a visualization exercise where you release yourself from having to worry about it anymore.

Turning Anxiety into Mindfulness

People who struggle with anxiety are actually blessed with a secret superpower. If they harness it, they are able to tap into an enormous potential for heightened conscious awareness. Every intrusive and anxious thought can be like a "meditation bell" calling you to awareness and bringing you back into the moment. How?

Try "mental noting." It's easy.

1. Become aware and observe yourself having thoughts. No judgment.
2. Note the experience and label it. "I'm thinking."
3. Keep going. Repeat until the thought dissipates or you move on.

Every time you have a thought, any thought at all, you can stop and remember to become aware of yourself. In some Buddhist temples and monasteries, a mediation bell rings periodically so that wherever people are and whatever they are doing at that moment, they can stop and reconnect to the present again. You can do the same with your own thoughts and self-talk. Every time you hear an anxious thought, treat it as a bell that has rung to remind you to come back to the present.

Of course, you won't be able to maintain awareness one hundred percent of the time, but if you can grab hold of an anxious thought and note it for what it is, then you can transform *any* thought into an opportunity to be mindful.

This technique is inspired by many different mediation techniques and is designed to quell distractions and calm down what the Buddhists call "monkey mind"—that inner chat that thoughtlessly leaps from one thing to another. Mental noting might not seem like much, but if you pepper your day with little moments of metacognition in this way, be prepared for big, big changes in the long run. Practice this often enough and you will find it much more difficult to become "fused" with negative thoughts. You simply maintain too much distance to ever get too tangled up.

Just remember three key elements when you practice mental noting:

Your **intention** should be to maintain awareness of the present moment.
Your **attention** should be on everything that is happening in the present only.
Your **attitude** should be non-directional, non-judgmental, and kind.

The classical approach during mediation is to say, for example, "There is hearing," or, "Hearing has happened," when you notice a dog barking outside. You might be really Zen and simply note, "Hearing." You don't allow yourself to run off and follow the hearing so that you are soon thinking, "That's the neighbor's dog," or, "I wish it would shut up." You simply note and label what your brain is doing, then move on.

In the case of anxiety, you do something similar to stop yourself from getting "distracted" by thoughts that seem urgent and important but really aren't. So if you're sitting at your desk, trying to work, and you notice a thought pop into your mind ("The performance review is going to be so awkward!"), you stop in your tracks, note the thought, label it, and move on without engaging. "Ruminating," you say, and pass it by.

Another way to bring in the principles of mindfulness to a brain that's hooked on anxiety is called "mundane task focusing." If you're one of the many people who dislike meditation or simply don't find room in their lives to practice it, don't worry—the Buddhists and meditators do not have the monopoly on mindfulness!

All that's required to calm an anxious mind is to remain in the moment. Anxieties and worries live *elsewhere*—they're in the past or the future. If you anchor right here and right now, though, your world slows down and becomes calmer and way more manageable.

1. Pick a mundane and everyday task that doesn't require too much brainpower—for example, washing dishes.
2. Do the task but do it very intentionally. Pay ultra-close attention to what you are doing. Focus on the bubbles of the soap. The temperature of the water. The rhythmic movement of your hands, and the weight of each dish as you hold it (as you can see, this is a form of grounding).
3. When your mind wanders, pull it back to the task at hand. Commit every last ounce of your attention to the task unfolding before you, nothing more.

You can find immense relief from overthinking and worry by doing completely ordinary everyday tasks, like walking to the post office or filling the car with fuel.

Summary

- We need distress tolerance skills to help us cope with extremely trying or painful moments, or emergency situations. When we're distressed, it's easy to slip back into old patterns of behavior or default to clumsy, destructive, or unconscious ways of coping—these are false coping mechanisms.
- Self-soothing is a way to acknowledge and accept pain that is inevitable—without making it any bigger than it should be. It is not distraction or avoidance, but about anchoring in the present using your five senses—a technique called grounding.
- TIPP stands for temperature, intense exercise, paced breathing, and paired muscle relaxation, all of which can help lower physiological arousal. Try cold water, vigorous movement, or breathing exercises to calm the limbic system.
- Practice radical acceptance, which doesn't mean we like what is happening, only that we have agreed to not fight with reality. Acknowledge how you feel and the reality of the situation and remind yourself of what matters.
- The ACCEPTS acronym (Activities, Contribute, Comparisons, Emotions, Push away, Thoughts, and Sensations) can help you better tolerate momentary distress—although not for the longer term.

- With anxiety, our goal is not to force ourselves not to worry, but to worry more efficiently. Scheduling worry time puts you in proactive control and helps you gain distance.
- Notice the anxiety, write down the time you'll postpone to—with the duration and content—then follow through as agreed.
- Mental noting and focused mundane tasks can help you turn anxious moments into opportunities for mindfulness.

Chapter 4: Upgrade Your Psychological Toolkit with Stoic *Amor Fati* Philosophy

Long before the first psychiatrists and psychologists began to make their models of human suffering, the ancient Stoics had a fully developed understanding of the human condition and a philosophy of living they believed to be the most balanced and rational. The fact that so many modern people still find solace and strength in these ancient principles is a testament to how useful they really are.

The Stoics were masters at "living in the present." They saw clearly that the answer to negative thinking and especially anxiety and worry was to come back to the only place you actually have any control: the present. The past matters, but it should be studied and learned from—then forgotten. The future also matters, but we should not obsess uselessly over it; instead, we should use what we have right now to make plans to prepare for the worst and set in motion projects that will serve us best. Beyond that, the future, too, should be forgotten—after all, it will arrive in due course one way or another!

Beyond Radical Acceptance: Amor Fati

One way of rethinking your relationship to the past is to adopt the Stoic attitude of *amor fati*. This translates roughly to "love of one's fate" and is a sentiment that is sadly not common in modern hearts and minds. With this attitude, one does not merely tolerate one's fate but embraces it—loves it. **Whatever happens in life—and that includes all the painful, confusing, and difficult parts—is welcomed and appreciated as something beautiful and, in its way, necessary.**

In his book *Enchiridion*, Epictetus advises us, "Do not seek for things to happen the way you want them to; rather, wish that what happens happens the way it happens: then you will be happy." In other words, learn to want what is, and you cease to fight against anything. He tells us in a later work *The Art of Living*, that "prudent people look beyond the incident itself and seek to form the habit of putting it to good use."

In his famous work *Meditations*, much-loved Stoic philosopher Marcus Aurelius says, "Universe, whatever is consonant with you is consonant with me; if something is timely for you, it's neither too early nor too late for me. Nature, everything is fruit to me that your seasons bring; everything comes from you, everything is contained in you, everything returns to you." Can you feel the enormous sense of *relief* in that passage?

These philosophers suggest that we quietly bear our misfortunes and be strong, but they are taking it somewhat further—our misfortunes, with the attitude of *amor fati*, are in fact not things to bear and endure and tolerate, but things to embrace. If reality itself has seen fit to make certain things occur, who are you to argue? In fact, why should you do anything other than be *glad* that events have unfolded in the way they have?

This way of thinking takes some time to digest since it is so radically different from the typical sense of regret, dissatisfaction, and resistance most of us are taught to eliminate when it comes to our lives. Though the original principles came from Stoic philosophers like Seneca and

Aurelius, it was also the philosopher Friedrich Nietzsche who revived the theme in his book *Ecce Homo*, saying, "My formula for greatness in a human being is *amor fati*: that one wants nothing to be different, not forward, not backward, not in all eternity. Not merely bear what is necessary, still less conceal it—all idealism is mendacity in the face of what is necessary—but *love* it."

This is a profound paradigm shift. What do you think your life would be like if you genuinely wanted "nothing to be different" and embraced every event—past, present, and future—as something marvelous? This sentiment goes beyond accepting what is (and the Buddhist philosophers would certainly understand this point)—it is about being decidedly enamored with *all* the shapes and contours of one's own life.

Nietzsche continues in his book *The Gay Science*,

"I want to learn more and more to see as beautiful what is necessary in things; then I shall be one of those who makes things beautiful. *Amor fati*: let that be my love henceforth! I do not want to wage war against what is ugly, I do not want to accuse; I do not even want to accuse those who accuse. *Looking away* shall be my only negation. And all in all and on the whole: someday I wish to be only a Yes-sayer."

Here, Nietzsche hints at the enormous potential that the *amor fati* attitude can bring about. If we not only accept but love what is our fate, we give ourselves the opportunity to find, create, or amplify any possible beauty, meaning, and power in those events. We can transfigure and transform them. We go from being reactive strugglers against reality, always saying "no" to those who have gratitude, curiosity, and positivity built into everything they do, so that there is nothing that they cannot say "yes" to.

If all of this sounds overly abstract, don't worry. There are very simple ways to cultivate *amor fati* in your own life, right now.

Tip 1: Define the event as objectively as possible

Remember that a thing is only good or bad because of the perspective you're taking on it. What is a tragedy for one is a blessing for another—and completely neutral for a third. Try to look at events without the veil of your own resistance, judgment, or opinion spread on top of it. To do this, write down an account of the event in the plainest, most neutral terms you can imagine, as if you were an uninvolved third party watching from afar. Do not put any interpretations, emotions, or opinions into the mix. When you read this back to yourself, you will see how much more manageable it is.

Remember the following old Buddhist proverb:

> *A farmer and his son had a beloved horse who helped the family earn a living. One day, the horse ran away, and their neighbors exclaimed, "Your horse ran away. What terrible luck!" The farmer replied, "Maybe so, maybe not."*

> *A few days later, the horse returned home, leading a few wild horses back to the farm as well. The neighbors shouted out, "Your horse has returned and brought several horses home with him. What great luck!" The farmer replied, "Maybe so, maybe not."*

> *Later that week, the farmer's son was trying to break one of the horses, and she threw him to the ground, breaking his leg. The neighbors cried, "Your son broke his leg. What terrible luck!" The farmer replied, "Maybe so, maybe not."*

A few weeks later, soldiers from the national army marched through town, recruiting all boys for the army. They did not take the farmer's son because he had a broken leg. The neighbors shouted, "Your boy is spared. What tremendous luck!" To which the farmer replied, "Maybe so, maybe not. We'll see."

Tip 2: Have a mantra

Jocko Willink is an ex-Navy SEAL and an author, and his mantra for all difficult or unpleasant situations is simple: "Good." He says,

> *"When things are going bad: Don't get all bummed out, don't get startled, don't get frustrated. No. Just look at the issue and say: "Good." Now, I don't mean to say something trite; I'm not trying to sound like Mr. Smiley Positive Guy. That guy ignores the hard truth. That guy thinks a positive attitude will solve problems. It won't. But neither will dwelling on the problem. No. Accept reality, but focus on the solution. Take that issue, take that setback, take that problem, and turn it into something good."*

Whatever mantra you choose, say it out loud to yourself when you catch yourself feeling decidedly not in love with your fate.

"Okay."

"Thank you."

"So it is."

"Yes."

"I welcome it."

Tip 3: Focus on action, focus on solutions

It would be a big mistake to assume that loving one's fate is the same as being a passive, defeated fatalist. In fact, the opposite is true; only when you fully and completely embrace what is can you properly engage with your full range of choice, agency, and power. We should love what is—but that doesn't mean we forfeit our chance to have a say, take action, and attempt to influence that reality.

When we love a challenge, we transform it into an opportunity.

When we love our flaws and weaknesses, we start to see that they open doors to our evolution and growth.

When we love our enemies, we can begin to see them as teachers.

When we love our tragedies, accidents, and losses, they begin to feel to us like gifts.

Take a look at the problem you've described and ask about your scope to change it. Think of what you can do, break that task down into smaller chunks, and then commit to taking the very next step, right now if possible.

If we only ever resist adversity, say "no" to reality, and fight against it, all those potential gifts, opportunities, lessons, and insights are lost. When you really think about it, is it such a wonderful thing to always get what we think we want? Do we *really* want to live in a world where we are never challenged, never uncomfortable, never surprised or humbled?

Negative Visualization

The Stoics called this technique *premeditatio malorum.* Modern motivational speakers and self-help gurus warn against entertaining the worst possible outcomes or dwelling on negativity, but for the Stoics, this activity actually had some value.

The idea is that you **occasionally spend a short amount of time imagining in detail the**

negative things that could happen in life. By doing so, you generate a renewed appreciation for all the things you do have. It's like you recalibrate, remembering what's important and putting your current concerns and worries into perspective as you find more gratitude for what is already working well for you. More than this, though, negative visualization is intended to put you back in control and take the sting out of worries and anxieties. When we insist on avoiding any negative premonitions at all, we don't give ourselves the chance to plan and prepare for them, and in a way, we give them more power over us.

In his 45 BC text *Tusculan Disputations*, Cicero explains, "I am ready to borrow of the Cyrenaics those arms against the accidents and events of life by means of which, by long premeditation, they break the force of all approaching evils. And at the same time I think that those very evils themselves arise more from opinion than nature, for if they were real, no forecast could make them lighter."

In his letters to Lucilius, Seneca echoes this sentiment by saying, "He robs present ills of their power who has perceived their coming beforehand." Elsewhere, he writes,

> "I will conduct you to peace of mind by another route: if you would put off all

worry, assume that what you fear may happen will certainly happen. Whatever the evil may be, measure it in your own mind, and estimate the amount of your fear. You will soon understand that what you fear is either not great or not of long duration."

But this technique is not just for use when times are tough, but when things are going well, too. In *Epistles* 18.6, he says,

> *"It is in times of security that the spirit should be preparing itself to deal with difficult times; while fortune is bestowing favors on it then is the time for it to be strengthened against her rebuffs. In the midst of peace, the soldier carries out maneuvers, throws up earthworks against a non-existent enemy and tires himself out with unnecessary toil in order to be equal to it when it is necessary. If you want a man to keep his head when the crisis comes, you must give him some training before it comes.*

In other words, if we wish to be mentally tough and resilient, we need to train ourselves to endure possibly negative outcomes, just as an athlete trains themselves to be strong in the face of physical adversity. Granted, the Stoic mindset can seem a little alien at times, and their advice may sound strange to modern ears. Exactly *how* can you apply negative visualization in your own life—and how is it different from simply catastrophizing?

Think of the aim of the exercises as three-fold. When you practice negative visualization, you are:

Increasing gratitude for what you have right now.

Desensitizing yourself to adversity and increasing your tolerance and resilience to it.

Allowing yourself to prepare for negative outcomes.

To hit all three aspects, here's an exercise to try.

1. Start by writing down one to three things that are very valuable to you, whether they're material things like a house or a laptop, or something abstract like a relationship, good health, talents, or time. This can also work well if you pick something that is currently causing you trouble.

2. Once or twice a week, sit down somewhere quiet to meditate for five minutes on what your life would be like

without these things. How would you feel? Explore the scenario in detail, pulling no punches.

3. Then, dig deep and imagine what mental, physical, and emotional resources you could draw on to deal with such a loss. In what ways might you be able to survive?

4. Finally, end the exercise by thinking of a few ways you could minimize the loss of such a thing, should it ever happen for real. After you contemplate loss in this way, is there something in your present behavior that needs to change? End your meditation session with a quiet moment, letting your fresh insights sink in and welcoming a sense of tranquility.

Let's consider an example. Eve is having a difficult time with her job. It's not the best fit for her and is causing a lot of day-to-day stress that frequently makes her consider quitting for something less intense. She begins to practice negative visualization twice a week, and one day, she picks "my job" as something to meditate on. She has been in the habit of thinking negatively about this job for months now, but for five minutes, she does the opposite and considers what would happen if she suddenly lost this job tomorrow.

She explores the feelings that come up. There's relief, yes, but she also realizes that the sudden lack of salary would be terrifying, and that she'd have to hunt for a new job—also an awful prospect. She pictures herself walking around her flat with little to do during the day, and imagines how she'd have to tighten her belt with spending until she secured another position. She can also see, though, how she'd cope—she knows that with effort, persistence, and drawing on her various networks, she *could* find a new job, one way or another.

When she comes out of her meditation, she has a new, subtler perspective on the issue. Though the problems are all still there, she is able to actually be grateful for the job, warts and all, and sees that her position is not so bad as she thought it was. She decides to take action. She *will* quit her job, but she will do so strategically. She commits to getting her resume up to scratch and start looking for possible positions, all without leaving the comfort of her current job just yet. The next day, all the same work stresses and irritations are there, just as they were before, but Eve is less bothered by them, more assured about her own ability to manage any outcome, *and* actively shaping a future outcome she'd most prefer.

Stoicism and CBT Combined—the "What-If" Technique

A useful CBT technique is inspired loosely by the spirit of Stoic negative visualization and is an interesting approach to use in the face of negative thinking, anxieties, and worries. The process is simple but powerful:

Step 1: Write down a future event or potential outcome that is causing you some anxiety.

Step 2: Then ask yourself the following questions:

"What if this were actually true?"

"What is the worst that could happen . . . and is that really so bad?"

Write down the answers to this question—including any negative thoughts and worries that it inspires.

Step 3: In response to these new fears, ask the same questions again. Repeat the process on *those* answers, and so on. Keep going until you arrive at a core fear and realize that it would not in fact be the end of the world.

For example:

Step 1:

"I'm worried I'm never going to meet anyone."

Step 2:

"What if this were actually true? What is the worst that could happen?" Answer: "If I never met anyone, I'd have to live the rest of my life alone without a partner. I'd never find anyone to love."

Step 3:

"You'd never have anyone, you'd be alone, etc. What if all of this were actually true?" Answer: "I'd be devastated! It would mean that I was totally unloved. I'd miss out on a big part of life."

Step 3 again:

"You'd be devastated, unloved, and missing out on a big part of life . . . so what if that were really true? Would it really be that bad?" Answer: "Well, it wouldn't be the absolute *worst* thing that could ever happen. But it would be pretty bad. I'd have to go to events on my own, live alone in a house . . ."

"Living alone in a house . . . is that really that bad?" Answer: "Well, I guess it's not the end of the world."

Often, when we're trying to make ourselves feel better, we may inadvertently run away from, deny, or avoid our fears instead of facing them head on so that we can see that they are not actually as serious as we've told ourselves they are. Take a look at the worst thing you can imagine—is it really that bad? *Really?* With this technique, we stop running and turn around to face our fear instead. What is the actual shape and size of this fear? Is it the end of the world even if it is as bad as you guessed?

Hidden in the core of many anxious beliefs is a deeper belief that "I can't cope" or "I can't bear it." But this is usually not true. People can and do cope with all sorts of things! It's not what you prefer, and it's not what you want. But it's doable. It can be managed. If you subtly change the way you think about it, it can even be reframed as something of value. Do this exercise and you'll realize that "living all alone in a house" is actually a secret fantasy of many coupled people. They might do the very same exercise as you but begin with the terrible fear they can't cope with: "I never get to be on my own or have my own space..."

When this technique is combined with *amor fati* and a little negative visualization, the "problem" can take on all sorts of interesting new dimensions. You start to open up to all the ways that you actually *love* living alone on your own terms and that, in its own way, never finding anyone to love is simply one more thing that gives color and flavor to your unique and beautiful life. Some of the world's most fascinating, accomplished, and self-actualized people never partnered up. Not *despite* their lack of life partner, but in many cases, *because* of it.

Consider what would have happened if you instead refused to entertain any negative premonitions about this fear. If you instead said to yourself, "I refuse to be anxious about this; I *will* meet someone one day," and spent your time on guided visualizations where you picture yourself meeting your soul mate. What then? Well, you might meet someone. But what if you don't? Your "positive visualization" has then left you with enormous expectations and very few resources to deal with their disappointment. By not engaging it, the fear becomes bigger. Besides, the person with a fear of being alone who is temporarily in a relationship has not genuinely addressed that fear—just *masked* it. The moment they find themselves alone again, they will find the fear is still there, just as it always was.

So the question is, who has the most mastery over their fear—someone who quickly finds a way to run away from it, or someone who can look squarely at it and not be afraid anymore?

"Remember that You Must Die"

Speaking of fears, let's dive into what is arguably humankind's biggest one: death. *Memento mori* is Latin for: "remember that you will die." How would you live your life if you knew that at the end of this week, it would all be over for you? Well, you'd probably be unwilling to waste a single moment and would take extra special care to live well—whatever that means for you.

You wouldn't get hung up on the opinions of people you don't care about.

You wouldn't struggle through difficult books because everyone else thought they were good.

You wouldn't tolerate bad behavior from those around you.

You wouldn't continue in a pointless job that didn't make use of your talents.

Here's the truth, though: this little thought experiment is not an experiment at all. **You really will die**. No, not at the end of the week (if you're lucky . . . although, what proportion of people who are reading these words right now won't be so lucky?). But eventually. Sooner than you think, most likely.

The intention with remembering this is not to make you depressed or defeated. Quite the opposite. It's to invigorate you; to inspire you to grasp, with fearsome gratitude, the miracle of your life right now; and to remind yourself that once this life is over, it's over. If we have dreams and desires, the time to make them happen is now. If we have fears and vices controlling us, the time to unshackle ourselves from them is now. Because, one day in the future, it is an absolute guarantee that we will no longer have the time to do either.

Tomorrow, when you wake up, remind yourself that you are alive. When you go to bed, remind yourself that you do not have infinite nights like these, and one day, you will lie down for the last time. In the novel *All the Light We Cannot See*, author Anthony Doerr says, "Open your eyes and see what you can with them before they close forever." If time is limited, don't you want to find a way to make all your worries, adversities, and problems *mean* something? If time is limited, don't you want to live in such a way as to squeeze every last drop out of the pleasures you have been gifted?

What is Your Orientation: Solution or Problem Orientation? Thought or Action?

Imagine a group of four friends is traveling together, but as they assemble at the airport, they realize that one of them has forgotten his passport at home. In the time it would take him to go back home, fetch it, and return, the plane will have already left. The group erupts into anxious chatter.

Friend 1: "I can't believe I've done this! I'm such a moron. I'm so sorry! I had no idea, really. I've never done something like this before. Oh man, what are we going to do? This is awful."

Friend 2: "It's okay. It's not your fault. You probably were just rushed when you packed this morning. Do you remember where you might have left it?"

Friend 3: "We're not going to make it. We can't go home now; he'll make us all late. No way he can come with us now. It's impossible. We'll be late."

Friend 4: "I've had a look online and there's a flight leaving two hours after this one. It'll cost 150 dollars to switch flights, but we still have time to do that. We three can go ahead and meet you on the other side?"

Each of us has a unique way of looking at life—and it goes beyond "negative" or "positive." Some of us focus on problems (like Friend 1 and Friend 3), others on how the problem came to be and its details (Friend 2), and still others focus on solutions (like Friend 4). In the above example, though, all four friends are facing the *same* issue—it is their response to it that makes all the difference.

Problem-focused thinking zooms in on what's wrong.

Solution-focused thinking zooms in on what *could* be right.

In our example, Friend 1 and Friend 3 are only looking at the fact of the problem. And the result is that they complain, express negativity, or blame one another. They hold on to the negativity feeling associated with the situation . . . and keep on holding on to it! They exclaim again and again how stupid it was to leave a passport at home, how bad it would be if they missed the flight, how unfortunate the whole thing is . . .

But Friend 4 is not looking at all this. They're looking at **solutions** and **actions**. What can be done?

Let's be clear: In this example, both interpretations are possible. There's no doubt that this *is* a frustrating and terrible situation to be in. Friend 4, however, isn't oblivious to these things—they're just not focused on them. Likewise, it's not that Friend 1 or Friend 2 can't agree that there's probably a solution to their problem—they're choosing in this moment not to focus on it.

You can probably see that the big difference between being problem-focused and solution-focused is acceptance of reality. Friend 4 has essentially said to themselves, "Yes, the whole thing is annoying . . . but we can't change that now, and dwelling on it won't bring us closer to fixing the problem."

Once you start becoming aware of problem-focus, you will suddenly see it *everywhere*. This attitude is sadly too common, with many people unconsciously defending their negativity by saying, "I'm just being realistic." Here lies a real danger: being firmly problem-focused while incorrectly assuming that you are solutions-focused. You believe, in other words, that your negativity and dwelling on the problem *is* how the problem gets solved.

Be Honest with Yourself

Do you have a problem-oriented attitude? Most people who do don't *think* they do. Radical honesty is a must. Have you ever said, "Why is this happening to me?" or complained about how unfair something is? Do you ever go on at length about what you *wish* was the case (but clearly isn't)? Do you even consider yourself uniquely unlucky or that there is something about you in particular that elicits a bad outcome from the universe at large? Chances are, you are predominantly problem-focused.

Problem-focus (or "out of power" language as discussed above) is passive, reactive, and negative by definition. It often shows itself in a few characteristic ways:

1. Asking "why?" of a problem
2. Complaining
3. Assuming a victim role
4. Blaming others
5. Self-pity
6. Framing things in terms of "fairness"

For example, you get on the scale one morning and discover that you've gained ten pounds over Christmas. Big problem. With a problem-focus, you think, "Why is life so unfair? Why is everything that makes you fat so delicious?! It's all that garbage everyone pushes you to eat over Christmas . . . with my bad metabolism, I never stood a chance. And now I look awful in my clothes... I just can't believe it..."

Can you hear the refusal to accept reality in the above? Do you also notice that there isn't really an answer to the question, "Why is life so unfair?" It's a bad question. In fact, it's not a question at all, but a complaint, and it makes several poor assumptions—mainly that life *is* unfair. If the unfairness of life is your starting position, you are framing yourself as a poorly treated victim and concluding that there is nothing to be done about it... except whine. This immediately shuts you off from your own agency and from a very obvious fact: You can lose the weight if you try.

However, having a solutions-focus is not about magically seeing a million ways to fix a problem—it's more the frame of mind that believes that *there is a solution* in the first place. Being solutions-oriented doesn't mean you instantly become a formidable problem-solver, barging through life's obstacles with ease. It simply means you are open enough to ask, "What can I do here?" and to follow through on that.

By the same token, being problem-focused is not always a bad thing. Problem-focused people are good at analyzing situations and seeing exactly where a breakdown has occurred, and why. However, unless they eventually move into solutions-focus, they will continue to dwell on the problem indefinitely and never give themselves the chance to convert their insight into action and to change things. Being too solutions-focused may mean that you lack nuanced understanding of the problem, and race in to fix things that you don't really grasp, just because you can't bear facing the discomfort of the problem for too long.

So, it's a question of balance:

Thinking about a problem is useful, but it needs to be combined with concrete **action**.

Noticing, understanding, and analyzing the **problem** is a valuable thing to do, but only if it's combined with a focus on the **solution**, too.

For an extremely problem-focused person, everything they look at is a problem, and even if they're offered a solution, they can instantly identify what's wrong with it. (Have you ever played a game of "yes, but…" with someone who was determined not to have you solve their problems for them?)

On the other hand, for an extremely solutions-focused person, everything looks like a solution—including things that really aren't.

What's worse is that they may be so keen on finding a quick fix that they skip over the part where they analyze and understand the problem they're supposed to be fixing. You've probably met someone like this before—there is a constant and almost frantic hopping from one promising idea to the next without stopping to understand the problem better first.

Because this is a book about the question of negative thinking and how to overcome self-sabotaging thought patterns, there's a good chance you struggle more with being overly problems-focused rather than too solutions-focused. So for now, we'll ignore that possibility and look at how to be less problem-focused.

What is your attitude to problems? Do you instantly throw your hands up and get angry or defeated, wondering why life has dealt you this blow? Do you get so focused on negative feelings that you become obsessed with them, unable to see beyond them? Do you go into victim mode and unconsciously hope that someone else will come and rescue you somehow?

These are difficult questions, and the way we individually face problems is a complex topic. We may have learned this behavior as children when our core beliefs about ourselves and our capacities were laid down. We may have had formative experiences that taught us not to expect too much or to have little faith in our own problem-solving abilities. More broadly, we may simply have the attitude that life is bad and difficult and unfair, so when a problem occurs, our response is more or less, "So what else is new?"

For now, one important theme is to remember that **negativity is a perspective**. It's not truth, but a particular view on the truth. And this view is one that is chosen... which means a different point of view can be chosen! The next time you feel yourself facing a problem, try the following Stoic-inspired exercise to help you acknowledge the problem without letting yourself get distracted from the task of finding a solution—if there is one.

Keep It Simple with the Two-Column Exercise

The Stoics believed that those things in life that cannot be changed must be borne with dignity and fortitude, but that it is also our duty to do our best to work at those things we *can* change. Resilience and strength, but never resignation and passivity. You might have seen this sentiment echoed in the Serenity Prayer, which goes,

"Grant me the serenity to accept the things I cannot change, the courage to change the things I can, and the wisdom to know the difference."

We can apply this to our own lives every time we face a problem by using a two-column technique. It's simple to do. Take a piece of paper and draw a line down the middle to create two columns. Label one "things I can change" and the other "things I cannot change." Now, spend a few moments thinking about the issue that is bothering you and (honestly!) assign its various aspects to one column or the other.

If you like, you might choose to do a kind of "brain dump" beforehand just to tease out all the elements of your problem. This is also an excellent practice to combine with any CBT techniques, or exercises where you're fleshing out your core beliefs.

Once you have thoroughly dissected the problem this way, it's time to start processing. Recall the skills of radical acceptance and *amor fati*—you will need this attitude when dealing with things in the "cannot change" column. Unless you apply a degree of acceptance and embrace what is, you risk getting trapped in a problem-focused loop, complaining, blaming, or acting the victim.

For things you *can* change, you will need a solutions-focused approach, and to switch your mode into action. For things in this column, ask yourself the following questions:

What can I practically do to address this problem?

What do I need to prepare or plan for?

What is the first step I need to take?

What do I need to learn?

Who do I need to ask for help?

How can I remove the current obstacle standing in my way?

How can I break the bigger task into smaller ones so that I can act right now?

You may discover that you prefer to have *three* columns: one for what you cannot control, one for what you can, and a third column for things that you have partial control over. The rest of the process is similar: Ask yourself what can be done and then commit to taking actions toward that goal. That portion that is not in your control can be let go, while you can carefully extract the portion that you can do something about—even if it's just a small thing.

Let's return to our earlier example of discovering that you've gained weight over

Christmas and aren't too happy about it. Your two-column list may look like this:

Things I can't change

The fact that I have gained ten pounds

What I did and what I ate in the past

Things I can change

What I eat and what I do now and in the future

How I talk about the problem and how I talk about myself

As you look at the second list, the next actions to take are obvious: commit to eating better, exercising, and refusing to blame anything or anyone else for choices you made in the past. For the things you can't change, well, it's worth spending the time to acknowledge that yes, you have gained weight and yes, it's probably your own fault—but don't dwell on it. Negativity is "useful" only in the sense that it creates insight that drives us to evolve. Learn what lesson you can, then move on. You serve nobody by beating yourself up or getting obsessed with guilt, shame, blame, or regret.

A variation on this exercise is even quicker. Identify what it is that you want, and then ask yourself, **"Is what I'm doing, thinking, or feeling bringing me closer to that?"**

If you're overweight and unhappy about it, then you probably want to lose weight. Notice yourself blaming Christmas, complaining about your metabolism, or focusing on how bad you feel in your clothes . . . and ask if any of it brings you closer to losing weight and being happier with yourself. No? Then it's useless. Have the serenity to just let it all go. Instead, become curious about the kind of things you'd feel, do, and think if you were someone who was losing weight right now . . . then do that. Yes, it will take courage.

In the end, it's not that being solution-focused in always superior to being problem-focused. Rather, as the Stoics understood, it's about the *wisdom* of knowing when to apply one and not the other, and in what proportion.

Summary

- The ancient Stoics were masters of living in the present.
- One way of rethinking your relationship to the past is to adopt the Stoic attitude of *amor fati*. This translates roughly to "love of one's fate." Whatever happens is embraced, wanting "nothing to be different." To practice it, look at events as neutrally as possible and then respond to them with a simple mantra like "good." By focusing on

action and solutions, we are able to transform adversity.
- Negative visualization is where we occasionally spend a short amount of time imagining in detail the negative things that could happen in life. This renews appreciation and gratitude for what matters, allows us to prepare for the future, and creates psychological resilience.
- With the "what-if" technique, we write down a fear and ask, "What if this were true?" and explore the worst that could happen, showing ourselves that it is tolerable and not so bad after all. Likewise, remember *Memento mori*, Latin for, "remember that you will die" to help remind you of what matters.
- Problem-focused thinking zooms in on what's wrong. Solution-focused thinking zooms in on what *could* be right and looks to taking action to change the situation. Thinking needs to be balanced with action. Focus on the problem needs to be balanced with focus on the solution.
- Remember the Serenity Prayer and try the two-column exercise to help you identify what you can change and what you can't. Accept what you can't, act where you can.

- Ask what you want and value, then ask yourself, "Is what I'm doing, thinking, or feeling bringing me closer to that?"

Chapter 5: Avoid the Trap of Toxic Positivity and Feel your Feelings

Craig is someone who has really turned his life around. In his early twenties, he suffered terribly from depression, anxiety, and low self-esteem. But that was before he joined a community yoga class and felt so much better that very same day. Within a few years, he was reading countless fascinating New Age self-help books, taking classes on the law of attraction manifestation, and had become a vegetarian. He grasped what he felt was an unavoidable truth: *As you think, so shall you become.*

To Craig, the universe was pure consciousness and love—if you could match that frequency of trusting and generative positivity, then you would always align with the good that was flowing all around you at all times. If you're negative, though, the universe will mirror that negativity straight back at you. In time, Craig starts to understand all the adversity that he'd experienced as a manifestation of his own lack of self-love and his own doubt in universal abundance.

And thinking this way worked for him. Until it didn't. When his sister died, Craig was completely bowled over by an unmanageable mass of negative feelings that caught him off guard. He told himself that there are no mistakes in life, that she was somewhere better, that it was all okay, and that there was no need to mourn since energy never disappears—it only changes form ... And yet, he still felt devastated. He hid these feelings of devastation, even from himself. He couldn't admit that part of his new conversion to the light meant obsessively guarding against any experience of the dark.

He put on a brave face, and when people asked how he was doing, he responded with speeches about the transcendental nature of mortality and the Tibetan Book of the Dead and how he was ecstatic to receive this lesson in non-attachment. In response to the mourning of his other family members, he remained aloof and occasionally sent them "inspiring" quotes that actually upset them. One day, he makes his mother cry when he not-so-subtly suggests that her continued upset is evidence of her poor spiritual development, and that she should meditate more instead of moping around. It sounds cruel, but it's only a natural conclusion of the very same philosophy that had helped Craig up till that point.

Craig's only crime was that he sincerely wanted to be *good*. Only good. He saw himself as strong and wise and happy. Who wouldn't want the same? And when he instead felt weak and foolish and desperately sad, he didn't know what to do with those feelings. When he spoke to his fellow New Age friends, and even when he consulted a local counselor, they only gave him pithy Zen koans or said, "Everything happens for a reason," or, "Try to remember the good times," unconsciously affirming this fear that negativity was unacceptable, and to indulge it to any degree meant that you were a bad person. For Craig, "bad" meant unenlightened, unevolved, and unintelligent. Things he really didn't want to be.

One day, a few months after the death of his sister, Craig is at rock bottom again. How did this happen? What about all that positive personal growth and development? What about all that positivity and enthusiasm—where did it go? He goes online to all the social media accounts that once gave him so much motivation and inspiration (did you know that Instagram has over fourteen million posts with the hashtag goodvibesonly?), and he only feels worse.

He again falls into a depression, not because he is mourning his sister's death, but because he sees his own mourning as something to be ashamed of. Everything feels worthless, imperfect, wretched. Craig looks at himself with hatred and thinks that he would be able to pull himself out of this misery if only he were more enlightened, more aware, more spiritually wise. But the truth is, Craig is in this mess **because** he sought out all these things in the first place—at the expense of acknowledging his authentic experience.

The Positive IS Powerful, But . . .
Toxic positivity is an overgeneralization of a positive and optimistic attitude. In a way, it's a cognitive bias because it refuses to acknowledge states of mind, events, thoughts, or feelings that are deemed "negative."

Positivity is a wonderful thing. This book would not exist unless there was some belief in positivity's power. Some would say that the most successful among us are not the pessimists or the realists, but those who encounter life with a *slight* glass-half-full approach. However, if you've encountered the "positive vibes only" brand of positivity in the self-help world, you've probably wondered whether this overly rosy view of the world is really the best approach to take.

Toxic positivity is actually pretty negative if you peek under the hood—**it's about denial, minimization, and invalidation . . . of your own experience. So, it's not positivity itself that is toxic, but our insisting that our genuine and real experience be something else.** Toxic positivity has us wearing masks, silencing our real feelings, and extending this invalidating attitude to others, too. As we see in Craig's case, the results are often the exact opposite of what we want.

The truth is, human beings are *complex wholes*. They contain both good and bad. Carl Jung once said, "I'd rather be whole than good." As the originator of the idea of the human shadow, Jung was fascinated by the psychic material we ignored, repressed, and disowned—where did it go? In Carl's case, the disidentified emotions just went underground until all that depression burst out and caused him to fall into a deep sadness.

There are lots of reasons we deny the "negative" parts of ourselves:

- We don't want others to think we're boring or unpleasant downers
- We don't want to cause others pain
- We don't want to admit that we are confused, mistaken, or flawed—i.e., our egos!
- We don't want to admit that we are frightened, weak, or vulnerable in any way
- We are worried that once we acknowledge negativity, it will flood us and we'll lose control

According to renowned shame author Brene Brown, these negative feelings are cultivated in silence, secrecy, and judgment. In Craig's case, his "positive thinking" came with a set of unspoken rules:

Silence: Don't admit that you are feeling distraught, even to yourself, and don't talk about it.

Secrecy: Hide the facts of this experience from everyone so it becomes your private torment

Judgment: Criticize yourself harshly for feeling this way

Craig cultivated a particular image of himself that he takes pride in. But secretly, he tells himself, "If they only knew what a total toxic and negative mess I really am, and if they really knew what a phony fake I am, they'd reject me for sure." Have you told yourself something similar? That you couldn't ever really reveal your true feelings to others for fear of the repercussions? *Understand that this is a judgment you have already made of yourself.*

The costs of denying our *full* experience (both positive and negative) are high. We live inauthentically and lose touch with what we really want, think, and feel—i.e., with who we really are! We feel isolated from others. Because we cannot open up in genuine vulnerability and truth with them, we never really connect, and so we feel even more alone in our shame.

What's more, we carry that attitude to others. We tell others to, "Think happy thoughts!" and what they actually hear is, "You can only be around me if you are also pretending to be this fake, eternally happy person." After all, if you can't bear your own negative feelings, how could anyone trust you to handle theirs with any care and tact? We end up attracting more inauthenticity. Our world gets increasingly more curated and controlled and *looks* happy, but feels emptier and emptier.

In the preceding chapters, we've worked hard to identify and root out distorted, unhealthy, and self-defeating thoughts and beliefs. But that doesn't mean you should replace all these with their polar opposites, glibly believing instead that everything is awesome, you can do absolutely anything you put your mind to, and that a fully actualized person is just brimming with joy and enthusiasm twenty-four-seven. Let's not allow the pendulum to swing too far in the other direction!

Good Versus Whole
Make your goal to be a person who **accepts** their complete, full selves, both dark and light.

It takes maturity to embrace what is, even though that may be imperfect, flawed, uncomfortable, or confusing. No human being is one hundred percent invulnerable. "Negativity" is built into the fabric of life itself—without it, we would never understand gratitude, we would never learn what we valued, we would never be challenged to improve, and we would never face the natural consequences of our behavior and the fact that not all choices are good for us. We are mortal. We can be hurt, we can make mistakes, and we can even be the "bad guys" sometimes.

To acknowledge all this is NOT to be negative any more than to deny it means we are positive.

The following sentiments are common whenever toxic positivity is in full swing. Notice if you use these phrases on yourself or with others, and gently challenge yourself to find room in there for your *real, full experience* instead:

"Stay positive!"—"How are you feeling, exactly? What is your experience like right now? I'm listening without judgment."

"Failure is not an option."—"Failure is learning. It's a part of life."

"It'll all be okay."—"What is happening for you right now?"

"Every cloud has a silver lining/Everything happens for a reason."—"Sometimes, bad things happen. What do you need to feel supported?"

"You got this!"—"I'm here for you no matter what. You deserve kindness and support even if you're having difficulty."

"Good vibes only."—"Ancient Roman Playwright Terence puts it best: '*Homo sum, humani nihil a me alienum put,*' which means: 'I am human, and I think nothing human is alien to me.' In other words, all vibes are allowed because they are

part of the rich, three-dimensional fabric of human experience."

Keep reminding yourself that toxic positivity does not have any benefits. It does not make life easier to bear, it does not guarantee more favorable outcomes, and it does not give you a kind of cheat code that allows you to bypass all the messy and uncomfortable parts of life. In fact, if anything, it makes the hard parts of life more difficult to bear. What we shove out of conscious awareness doesn't disappear. It only festers somewhere else, where it doesn't get the benefit of our compassionate awareness to help process it. Thus, the negativity that we don't acknowledge never has the chance to teach us or enrich our lives in any way—what is "positive" about that?

Letting Go of Toxic Positivity

Step 1: Make friends with discomfort

Toxic positivity is, at least at first, the easy way out. Facing your discomfort head on takes courage and honesty. If you notice yourself leaping in to reassure, dismiss, invalidate, or soothe a negative feeling, stop and notice what you're doing. Try to instead "sit with" your unpleasant emotion. Don't try to destroy, fix, dissolve, or triumph over it . . . but don't succumb to it, either. Just sit alongside it. Put a name to your feeling and leave it at that. Watch your mind try to run around everywhere to escape it, and bring it back to the present and to the truth of reality.

"I'm sad. I feel a deep, deep sadness about my sister passing away. I'm so confused and hurt." Then don't judge, interpret, or rush to fix what comes up. Just let that emotion be what it is.

Step 2: Be patient

Toxic positivity can feel like a quick fix and an instant relief. But working through your emotions takes time. Don't rush and be overly keen for a happy resolution, or barge ahead wanting to skip over the difficult bits so you can get to the happy ending where you've learned your lesson and can move on. Seeds sprout when they're ready, wounds heal as best as they can, and emotions come and go, but on their own schedule. Take it as your duty to give them comfortable passage—don't hold on to them but don't be too eager to rush them on, either.

"I'm sad right now. I don't know how I'll feel tomorrow. I know this won't last forever, but I'm willing to let it last as long as it needs to."

Step 3: Distinguish between productive and unproductive negativity

Finding a balance between positive and negative is not complicated. If there is a negative side to positivity, then there is a positive side to negativity. You can navigate your way through them both by framing it all in terms of productivity or usefulness:

<u>Productive negativity</u> – pure, authentic emotion that does not contain judgment, shame, or resistance to that emotion. Negativity that promotes insight, learning, resilience, or inspired action.

<u>Unproductive negativity</u> – the secondary negativity that emerges around an authentic emotion and serves to prolong and exacerbate it without any benefit. Negativity that limits options, inhibits action, and leads to passivity, despair, and loss of agency.

Let's go back to Craig and his example. When he looks at his second big bout of "depression," he can ask whether it's unproductive or productive. He may see that there are actually two emotions—one is sadness, and the other is a mix of shame, anger, and irritation *about* that sadness. The secondary emotions don't seem to go anywhere—in fact, they only seem to make him feel worse. But he also notices that when he focuses on the primary emotion—the initial sadness—it hurts, but if he doesn't heap judgment and shame onto it, it doesn't feel as bad as he thought it would.

In fact, once he fully acknowledges how he actually feels, he notices with surprise that he doesn't feel that way for long. His sadness, once acknowledged, actually spurs him on to feel new, different things. After a few weeks of "sitting with" how he genuinely feels, something else stirs in him: He wants to act. He feels compelled to do something meaningful in his sister's memory—something he wouldn't have dreamed of if he was still pretending that everything was okay!

Like so many people who learn to let go of toxic positivity, Craig understands that the remedy for depression is not happiness, but *authentic sadness*. Toxic positivity doesn't help, but neither does stagnant depression and despair. Instead, Craig finds a way out through the middle: by accepting what is so that it can be processed and released.

Step 4: Reconnect to your values and shift to problem-solving

Emotions exist for our benefit. They are there for a reason and have evolved to keep us safe, help us to connect, and allow us to live a life of meaning. Emotions—*all* emotions, even the awful, inconvenient, or embarrassing ones—can teach us something if we are willing to listen. It is not necessary in life to suffer needlessly just for the sake of it. Rather, you are a human being who is tasked with finding meaning and purpose in your experiences. If you can invoke your values and principles, you can imbue your suffering with meaning—and transform it into something beautiful.

As you accept and sit with uncomfortable emotions, try to look for the hidden blessing. Not in a "everything happens for a reason!" way, but in a way where you graciously make the best of everything that comes your way. Compare experiences against your values. For example, if you value independence and autonomy, allow a frightening cancer scare to teach you the value of interdependence and the power of asking for help. On the other hand, you might find that negative experiences with someone who keeps violating your boundaries confirm for you values that you never knew you had before—the principles of dignity and self-worth.

The trick is that you cannot be inspired and taught by negative emotions until you *feel them fully*. You cannot skip over the painful part and rush to the blessing in disguise part—the blessing is only revealed **by** enduring the negative emotion in the first place. Craig, for example, values intellectual mastery, truth, and spiritual development. But if he acknowledges his real emotions, they may teach him that, ironically, the best way to move forward sometimes is to go backward, and the best way to grow is to be willing to let go of your ego's idea of what life should be like.

Identify your personal values and the principles you hold most dear. And then let them inspire you to take action and solve problems. If you are going through a difficult time, remind yourself of what makes life meaningful for you. Then take action that incorporates the way you feel but brings you closer to what matters. For example, you may face the fact of deep regrets you have about your past. But you remind yourself that you **value** who you are today—and that person is who they are because of those past experiences. You take **action** and forgive yourself, vowing also not to act today in ways that you might regret tomorrow.

Think of negative emotions as a pathway into more deeply understanding your values—and bringing them to life in action. Ask yourself, **"How does a person who values what I value behave when they experience what I'm experiencing?"**

One Underappreciated Way to Genuinely Feel Better

Toxic positivity is not really about feeling good feelings—it's more about the *desire* to feel good feelings, or even the expectation and entitlement to those positive feelings. It's this unrealistic expectation that makes encountering real life even more unpleasant than it would ordinarily be! If we have a vision of what life should look like (do you catch the distorted thinking?), then we are at risk of labeling even normal or neutral events as "negative" when they aren't—they just don't match up to some artificial image of what we think positivity looks like. So, we may wake up one day to a completely normal and ordinary life, but because we are not super energetic and enthusiastic, our work doesn't light a fire in us, and we don't happen to be madly in love with our partners that day—we think something is wrong.

In a way, toxic positivity has an unfortunate side effect: it makes us ungrateful. We may be permanently dissatisfied if we compare our lives to an unrealistic vision of the glittering and eternal contentment we feel we're supposed to have. If you genuinely want to feel happier, though (right now, not when all your pesky problems are solved and you are finally perfect), then try to focus with gratitude on what you have.

It sounds too simple to work, but it does. Start every morning with a list of five things that you are grateful for in your life right now. Sometimes, we already have wonderful and positive lives—we've just become desensitized to our blessings and begun to take it all for granted. Right now, can you think of five things that are perfectly "ordinary" in your life that are, in fact, wonderful gifts?

Emotional Regulation
As we become better at recognizing negative and distorted thinking, and as we learn to guard against fake, unrealistic "positive thinking," we find that we are developing a skill that goes far beyond positive and negative: **emotional regulation.**

When we are capable of emotional regulation, we become conscious and capable masters of our own ever-unfolding emotional experience. We can reuse to engage in destructive or distorted thinking, while at the same time know when to tolerate and "hold" negative emotions, asking ourselves what good we can extract from them. We are likewise aware when we are feeling calm, content, joyful, hopeful—and welcome that too, being fully aware of how to cultivate and enjoy those emotions when they happen.

Consider the emotion of anger.

Is anger a "positive" or "negative" emotion? Well, it really depends.

If you're at work and dealing with an irritable customer, you cannot freely express your anger or let it get the better of you. Instead, you have to notice the anger, choose not to succumb to it, and act as professionally as you can.

However, if someone in your personal life insults you and attempts to violate a boundary, you would feel anger, too. In this case, though, expressing some of this anger may be exactly the right thing—since it clearly communicates your limits, asserts your dignity, and lets the other person know to back off!

Anger is a normal and natural emotion to have in both situations. However, in the first, it's much less useful to express it than in the second. In both these cases, there is a higher awareness that is taking control and asking, "What am I feeling? Why? What is the cause of this emotion, and what will be the effect of me acting on it? What do I want to achieve here? How can I help this emotion move on?"

This is the voice of emotional self-regulation. It is not merely a case of "upregulating the good feelings and down-regulating the bad ones," but rather a meat-emotion that allows you to be aware of and take charge of your emotional state—and then take action in a way that makes sense for you in any given context.

So, what makes an emotion "positive" or "negative" is a mix of

1. our own goals
2. our context
3. the values and principles we're living by

If we are not in control of ourselves, not aware, and not acting with a mind to our goals and values, then even if we feel "positive" emotions, we can't really be said to have mastered self-regulation.

First things first—emotional regulation is NOT the same as repression, toxic positivity, or ignoring how you really feel. Rather, it's about consciously choosing

- which emotions we pay attention to and encourage
- when we have them
- how we express them externally
- how we experience them internally

Note that there is no option to "choose whether I feel emotions or not." We all do! Emotions are a fact of life. But we do get a lot of say over when, where, and how we express them. We choose all the above in relation to our **goals and values**. For example:

On receiving a terrible birthday gift, "I choose not to express disappointment right now because I value my friendship with this person and don't want to hurt their feelings."

Before heading into an important job interview, "I choose to drastically dial up my feelings of confidence and enthusiasm so I can impress my interviewer because my goal is to get hired."

During some alone time with your journal on a Sunday morning, "I choose to explore and express my sadness right now because I want to process and release these feelings and grow as a person."

Goals and values provide a framework. Together with our awareness, they help us decide on the **intensity**, **quality,** and **duration** of our emotional response. So, we saw that Craig was in the grips of toxic positivity and was being emotionally inauthentic with himself and others. But what would it have looked like for him to demonstrate emotional regulation instead?

Intensity – Craig could have faced his sadness but altered how much of it to show to himself and others depending on the situation. He could have allowed himself to be completely vulnerable and expressive during therapy, moderately open with his friends, and honest but more guarded with his work colleagues.

Quality – "Sadness" is a pretty big emotion that contains lots of subtler shades and nuances, which Craig could play up or down depending on the situation. With his New Age yoga friends, he could express the bittersweet and wistful sides of mourning, but with his mother, engage more on the level of death being an incomprehensible injustice. With his therapist, he can focus on the raw, unapologetic feeling of grief and explore childhood memories of his sister. With a colleague, he can express a more formal sentiment. And so on. All these expressions are "real"—it's just that Craig is choosing for his own purposes to focus on each of them in different moments.

Duration – Craig can also put himself in charge of how long he engages his emotions. In conversation with a close friend, for example, he might allow himself to reveal plenty of vulnerable emotions, but he consciously chooses not to let this expression go on and on.

Instead, after a few minutes, he steps out of the limelight and allows his friend to talk, too.

If it seems a little weird to have so much control over your emotions, consider the fact that emotions themselves are often short-lived and context-dependent anyway. Remember that emotions are there for a reason and serve a function—there is nothing wrong with consciously stepping in and *choosing* what that function should be! Likewise, all emotions are brought into being through and with our cognitive evaluation and the activation of our core beliefs. This happens whether we realize it or not—so why not choose the core beliefs we want to guide this important process?

The Life Cycle of an Emotion
We can imagine that all emotions play out on a timeline:

There is (1) the initiating event or situation, followed by (2) our conscious attention on that event. This is followed by (3) our own unique appraisal of that event, and (4) it's this appraisal (not the event itself) that results in us feeling an emotion. From there, the emotion may die down naturally or be prolonged. It may prompt action, or it may get repressed and sent into "the shadow" ... perhaps to burst free at a later time.

So, for example, you have a long-haul flight booked for the following morning. You make an appraisal ("I hate flying! What if the plane crashes?"), and the resulting emotions are anxiety, panic, and fear.

We can step in to regulate our emotions at a few points in this process. Here's how it would look if you were trying to regulate the anxiety you faced when thinking about your upcoming flight:

Situation selection – This is where we choose which situations to enter according to the emotional outcomes we can expect for doing so (occurs *before* we encounter 1, the initiating situation).

In our example, this could look like simply avoiding situations we know will trigger and worsen panic. We decide not to watch an episode of *Air Crash Investigation* and deliberately avoid a friend who you know shares your anxiety and will only work you up into a froth if you talk to them too much before your flight. Another possibility is that, knowing how we'll respond, we avoid the trip entirely or find another way to get to our destination.

Situation modification – This is where we choose to change or alter the situation in some way (this is during 1, the initial situation).

In our example, let's say you do go on the flight. The situation can be modified to cause less anxiety, though. You take a mild tranquilizer and get an aisle seat and bring plenty of distractions as well as air-sickness medication if you need it. You practice breathing exercises and calming mantras.

Attentional deployment – This is where we choose to focus our attention on specific aspects of the situation (this is during 2, where we place our attention).

In our example, let's say you do get the flight, and despite your best efforts, you are still anxious. You consciously choose in that moment not to focus on and magnify the stress. Instead, you try to talk to the person next to you, play an immersive game, or try some challenging brain puzzles that take your mind off things—you only have a fixed mental bandwidth, and you'll have less available if you spend it all on another task!

Cognitive change – This is the choice to consciously modify the meaning we are ascribing to various aspects of the situation (this occurs at 3, when we make our appraisal).

In our example, the thoughts surrounding this flight might be very negative: "You can't avoid this, but it's unbearable." "You'll probably die." "You hate flying more than anything else in the world." But you can choose to make a different appraisal. You can reframe the situation like this: "I am being really brave facing my fears right now," or, "Ha ha, look at me! Isn't this silly fear of mine ridiculous?" or even, "Flying is annoying and uncomfortable, but it's far from the end of the world."

Response modulation – This is choosing to change the way we respond to our emotions physiologically, experientially, or behaviorally (this occurs at 4, the final response).

In our example, you still may find yourself enormously anxious. But you can still choose how you respond to this response itself. Let's say you notice your panic, but you are compassionate about it and accept it for what it is without judgment and resistance. Fearing a panic attack coming on, you call a flight attendant and discreetly explain the situation, asking if there is a private place onboard you can go for a few minutes to gather yourself.

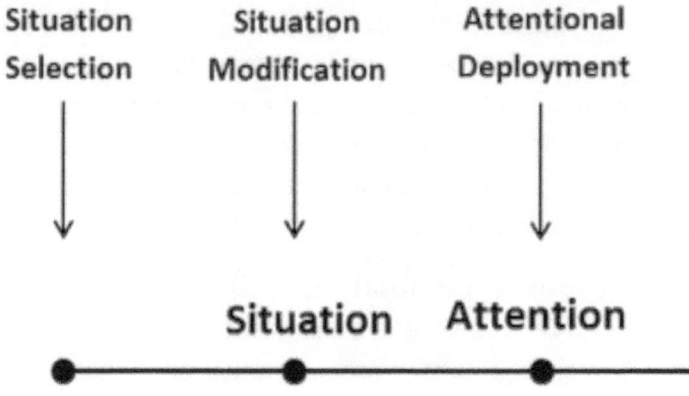

As you can tell, the point at which one aspect of the emotion ends and another begins is not clearcut, but this is not especially important. What is important is that you are aware and in control of the emotion as it unfolds, and taking steps to master that emotion at whatever stage that happens to be.

The above process may seem complicated when laid out all at once, but it's rather simple to learn it yourself. Here's how:

Step 1: Become aware

Ask yourself some of the following questions:

What am I experiencing?

Why am I experiencing it, or what came before?

Is this emotion helping or hindering me? What effect is it having overall?

What are my goals and values in this situation?

How does this emotion play into those goals and values?

Step 2: Consider context

Emotions don't occur in a vacuum. They're part of an unfolding situation in the external world and usually plugged into a social and physical environment. Look at the situation you're in and ask the following questions:

How does my emotion fit within this context?

Is any aspect of my situation changeable? How?

Can I make any changes that will help me achieve my goal or align with my values?

Step 3: Modify the situation

If the situation itself can't be changed, it can usually be shaped and modified somewhat. Become curious about how. Ask:

Would it be to my benefit to share my emotion with others?

If so, how best should I share it?

What changes to the situation would serve me best right now, given my goals and values?

Can I remove or introduce an object, a person, or an idea to change the dynamic in my favor?

Step 4: Put your focus where you choose

Don't just look at the situation, but look at how you're looking at the situation. What are you focusing on and what are you not paying any attention to? Become curious and notice what's happening both inside and outside your head, asking:

Where is my attention primarily going?

Is this focus helping or hindering?

Would it help me to focus on something different?

What is there currently in my situation that, if I focused on it, would help me increase positive emotions or reach my goal?

Is there anything that can distract me from a negative emotion right now?

Step 5: Modify the way you're appraising the situation

The way you are feeling is a direct result of how you are thinking about the situation. Once you become aware of how you're framing the situation, see if the following questions can bring some insight:

Is the current way you're thinking about this situation helping you achieve your goal?

Can both the emotion and the situation be looked at in another way?

Is it really that bad (i.e., have you correctly and usefully appraised the intensity of the emotion)?

Step 6: Modify how you're experiencing and expressing this emotion

The way you express your emotion will have an influence on the people around you, your environment, and the situation itself. Ask:

Do I want to share my experience—and if so, how?

If I don't wish to share it, how may I make that easier for myself?

What do I wish to change right now?

As you can see, with these questions, you are moving along the timeline of the emotion, looking for opportunities and areas along the way where you can intervene with action or reframing that speaks to your goals and values. You might do this *before* an anticipated situation, *after* the situation has already played out, or *during* the situation as it unfolds. Naturally, you will have more options the sooner you intervene. It's worth noting as well that it may be easier to take control the earlier along in the process you are. If the emotion is well underway, you may have to spend far more effort to modify it than if you had carefully avoided it in the first place. Prevention is always better than cure.

Not every situation will have an opportunity to make significant changes. Some situations will vary in how much you could possibly do at each stage. But, if you follow the above basic process, you are taking control of your emotional reality and steering it in the direction that suits you best, whatever the difficulties and limitations.

To recap:

1. Become aware of your emotion, your values, and your goals.
2. Consider your context and see how you are interacting with it

3. Take steps to change the situation
4. Notice where your attention is going and make changes
5. **Modify the way you're appraising the situation and the meaning you're giving it**
6. Take steps to change the way you are experiencing or expressing the emotion

As a brief example:

1. You become aware that you are experiencing fear and self-doubt after being asked to give a presentation the following day. You value bravery and confidence, and your overall goal is to do well at work.
2. You become aware of the context: You are well liked at work and being offered more responsibility. Your fear, however, might cause you to shy away from some of these opportunities.
3. You become aware of what you can change in the situation—you *could* refuse to do the presentation, but that may create a bad impression.
4. As you prepare, you notice that your thoughts tend to catastrophize. You deliberately steer your focus to other things—for example, the favorable reports you've received so far and

evidence from colleagues that you are doing a good job.
5. You deliberately choose to re-appraise the situation, going from: "This is a threatening and unpleasant event," to: "I am being given an exciting opportunity—how lucky for me!"
6. You decide to briefly confide in your boss, explaining your nervousness and asking for a day or two more to prepare the presentation. You express your fear very strategically, however, and express it only so far as to convey to your boss that you take the presentation seriously and want to do it properly (rather than treating the meeting as a mini therapy session!)

Usually, it is Step 5 that will have the most powerful impact, so if you can remember nothing of this process in the heat of the moment, try to remember to ask yourself simply, **"Is the way I'm thinking about this problem working for me right now?"** This alone will often open up doors of insight into other ways you can make modifications to the situation.

When we become good at mastering emotional regulation, we learn that our emotions are not in control of us—but it's not exactly true to say that *we* are one hundred percent in control of *them*, either. Rather, our emotions emerge as part of a broader situation, and they're caused and sustained by our beliefs and thought processes. Strictly speaking, we can never "control our emotions," but we can always take steps to control our environment, our thoughts, our reactions, and how we manage our emotions both internally and externally—which in turn will influence our emotions.

Summary

- Toxic positivity is a kind of cognitive distortion and is an overgeneralization of a positive and optimistic attitude. It consists of denial, minimization, and invalidation of your own experience. Toxic positivity grows with shame, silence, and judgment. Positivity itself isn't toxic, but denying our reality is. Human beings are wholes who contain both good and bad.
- We can embrace the *whole* instead of the *good* by watching the phrases we use, making friends with discomfort, being patient while we are in process, distinguishing between productive and unproductive negativity, and reconnecting to what we value and want to achieve in life. Ask yourself, "How does a person who values

what I value behave when they experience what I'm experiencing?"
- Keeping a gratitude journal is a great way to create genuine feelings of positivity.
- Rather than creating good emotions and getting rid of negative ones, we can practice emotional self-regulation and become conscious masters of our own ever-unfolding emotional experience.
- What makes an emotion good or bad is the context and our own goals and values. We regulate when we decide which emotions to attend to, when, how, and for how long.
- Emotions have a life cycle, and we can manage those emotions at any point in the cycle—before the situation, during the situation, with our attention, with our cognitive appraisal, and finally, with our emotional response. Generally, the sooner you intervene, the easier it is to modify the situation.
- Ask, "Is the way I'm thinking about this problem working for me right now?"

Chapter 6: But Where Does Negative Thinking Really Come From?

The more you work at identifying and rewriting your negative thought patterns, the better you'll come to understand this part of yourself—and realize how deep those roots really run. Why are some people so prone to negative thinking, pessimism, and a defeated attitude? Why do some of us dwell on anxieties and get embroiled in self-doubt, while others don't? Why do some people struggle with depression and low mood all their lives, while others seem to be functioning from a seemingly inexhaustible well of optimism?

These are big questions, and psychology has been trying to answer them for a long time. In this book, we've focused on possible answers at the psychological level—without getting too bogged down in overanalyzing what is in the past. We've explored how a critical and distorted inner dialogue encourages us to frame events according to a particular mental filter. And we've seen how thoughts and core beliefs influence the perspective we use to interpret everything around us. But then the question is, where did these thoughts come from? And what distorted those filters in the first place?

There are different levels at which we can think about the problem:

Physical – it's about hormones, genes, neurotransmitters, the food you eat, and the exercise you get (or don't)
Emotional – your unique feelings and responses to events that color and shape everything
Cognitive – the way you understand, explain, and conceptualize the world and yourself
Psychological – how your emotional and cognitive processing comes together into internal schemas and narratives
Social – the way your thoughts, feelings, and behaviors interact relationally with those around you, particularly your immediate family and early caregivers
Evolutionary – the fitness adaptations you've inherited from your ancestors
Cultural – the broader social and environmental significance of your life

Spiritual – the broader meaning of your life in relation to the divine or transcendental
Historical – your life as a developmental, and in the context of broader time scales relations
Political – the way your life interacts with the economy, the law, and the overarching power dynamics you live within

At *every* level, we can be influenced either toward a way of living that is predominantly pessimistic and negative, or one that supports our own conscious choice and agency. Though this book has focused mainly on the cognitive, emotional, and psychological dimensions, it doesn't take long to see that this is not the full story—if you were an impoverished peasant living in medieval times and suffered from malnutrition and disease all your life, it's hard to imagine how any of the techniques in this book could make a dent!

To return to the question of what causes a person's negative disposition—well, everything!

But the reason we've focused on the psychological/cognitive/emotional aspect is because, frankly, this is the area of life where we have the most control. In this final chapter, we'll look at two more sources of negativity and make an attempt to mitigate their impact on our daily life. The first is what's called "**negativity**

bias," and the second is the **power of relationships** to create or counteract negativity in our lives (specifically, how toxic relationships can create and sustain negativity). This expands our examination of negative thinking to include some evolutionary and social causes, respectively.

Your Negativity May Be "Hardwired"
Simply, the negativity bias is the human tendency to register and focus more readily on negative stimuli while ignoring or downplaying positive ones. It means that we tend to remember negative experiences more vividly than happier ones, dwell on insults more than we do on praise, perceive loss as more painful than we perceive gain as pleasurable, and give more mental airtime to negative thoughts than to positive ones. In other words, we have a bias for the negative. Research has uncovered all sorts of ways this bias pops up:

- We tend to assume that very negative news must be more true or real
- We tend to be more motivated to avoid a loss than to win a gain
- We even tend to make decisions based more on negative information and learn more effectively after negative experiences instead of positive ones

Think about finding a fly in your soup—everything else about your evening out at a fancy restaurant may be perfect, but that single tiny fly is likely to receive the bulk of your attention! On an otherwise great date, your brain focuses on that one embarrassing thing you said, or the spinach stuck in the other person's teeth. On a report card, you gloss over all the praise and dwell on the single criticism you received (remember the "discounting" cognitive bias?).

It turns out that this is not just a psychological phenomenon or a question of a bad attitude. It's not about personality. It's not a reaction to trauma or a personal failing or some strange, unique thing that only happens to you. Rather, the human predisposition to zoom in on what's wrong has evolutionary roots—nothing could be more ordinary or predictable. Those of our ancestors who focused more heavily on the negative had a survival advantage on those who didn't. If a person is hypersensitive to potential threats in the environment, they may have a lot of false positives, but when something genuinely is a case of life and death, they're likely to survive. Those who ignored or downplayed that threat, however, would likely not.

. . . But that Doesn't Mean It's Written in Stone

The Negative Nancys of the world, in other words, lived to pass on those genes that would bias their offspring to focusing on the negative more than the positive. This tendency is so hardwired that neuroscientists have found heightened activity in response to negative stimuli compared to positive ones—this is true even for very young infants.

But, while our bias for the negative may have evolutionary roots, **that doesn't mean that we are pre-destined to have this orientation for all time**. With awareness and conscious effort, we can mitigate, pre-empt, or challenge our knee-jerk biases and make sure that this primal part of ourselves doesn't get the last word. The negativity bias served our ancestors well and did indeed keep us safe and alert to threats in our environment. In fact, it *still* serves this function today.

But that doesn't mean that we can't engage with it, double-check it, and factor in our own higher, conscious choice on the matter, too. As human beings, we have ancient, inborn biological tendencies. We also have an incredible organ that no other animal possesses: a human brain. With this we can become aware, choose, learn, create, adapt, and make meaning.

The great thing about understanding the negativity bias is that you *know* that you are always primed to look at the worst in a scenario—so you can do something about it. It's not unlike the way your leg will reflexively bounce up when a doctor taps your knee in just the right place.

Imagine an ordinary person in an ordinary relationship whose partner does something wrong and hurts them. Instantly, they're put on the defensive as this insult expands in their awareness to take up all their attention. This single negative action soon starts to be all that they can see—the countless positive things their partner has done for years on end seem to vanish, eclipsed by the single negative one. This focus on the negative is a cognitive distortion. The person ends up saying things like, "You always do this," and, "You don't care about me," (hello, generalization and mind-reading bias!). This is exactly the same as saying that *no part* of the entire fancy restaurant experience was good simply because there was a fly in the soup.

Resentment builds, miscommunications abound, and the relationship ends. However, had this person understood the negativity bias and observed that their own thought processes were being heavily influenced by this tendency, things might have played out differently. They might have been able to say, "I'm really angry right now, and all I can see is the negative. What happened is bad, but I can also see that I'm fixating on it and that there are lots of good things in my relationship . . ." Consider how different conversations would be if the person held this attitude rather than unconsciously expecting and indeed seeking out the very worst in their partner.

But it's not just relationships where this bias plays out. Famed authors, researchers, and neuroscientists Kahneman and Tversky, in their Nobel Prize–winning work, explored the fact that people tend to place greater weight on the negative than the positive when making decisions. Their research helped them conclude that **people seem to fear loss more than they desire gain**—for example, people have a greater reaction to losing twenty dollars than to gaining twenty dollars.

This means that people often tend to prefer the status quo, even a negative status quo, simply because changing is perceived to incur too many potential losses—and the perceived gains are not enough to offset it. Negativity bias can influence our relationships, but it can also affect the way we process risk and reward.

As an example, we may be trying to make a decision between staying where we are or moving houses, or else keeping our job or accepting a new one. The thing is, we are not weighing up the options we have in a balanced, neutral way. Rather, we are placing more weight and emphasis on potential loss than we are on potential gain—and consequently we may stay in a suboptimal situation and miss out on good opportunities.

Here's an example. We might see that a new job pays twice as much and is way more fun but requires a month of intense training first, which we may potentially fail. We might also see that the current job doesn't pay much and is a bit boring but doesn't require any additional effort or take any risk. Objectively speaking, the new job is probably the better choice. But if we succumb to the negativity bias, we may overinflate the potential loss ("that month of training is just too risky!") and downplay the potential gain (a lot more money and more fun to be had), giving us a distorted picture of our options. **If we consciously recognize that the negativity bias is there, though, we can factor it in and make sure we're not unduly focusing on the negatives**.

Countering the Bias for the Negative

The good news is that you have already encountered (and hopefully tried) several powerful techniques for counteracting the human tendency to focus on the negative. Negative visualization and a gratitude journal especially can help you recalibrate so you are more aware of the good around you, not just the bad.

The solution is obvious—**if you cannot rely on your brain to automatically and unconsciously look for the positive, then you will have to *deliberately* draw your attention to it instead**. And it is there!

Pause to savor positive moments and register them fully. There is no evolutionary advantage to smelling the roses—but your life will be immeasurably improved if you can. Stay in the moment and relish all the lovely things that are actually happening all around you. If something positive is going on, literally imagine turning your mental antenna in its direction and paying it close attention. "This is positive. I'm enjoying this." Your mind will not do this for you—be deliberate instead and *choose* to see the good in things.

Mindfulness, presence, positivity, and gratitude all tend to go together. When we are conscious and awake to the moment—the full moment—we start to realize how fascinating and how lovely it is. And then we cannot help but feel grateful and content.

Try it tomorrow morning the moment you wake up.

Maybe you take a few seconds to really relish how comfortable your bed is, how soft the pillowcase. You stretch, and that long, taut feeling in your legs is just the most delicious thing ever. You yawn—that feels pretty good too, actually. You notice a pang in your stomach as you realize you have to get out of bed soon and go to work, a prospect you're dreading a little. But then you remind yourself of how you were unemployed a year ago, and how tense you were about money, and how it dented your self-esteem. This job isn't perfect, but you give yourself an internal pat on the back. You've made it this far, and you can keep going. You watch all that potential anxiety about your work just pass by. You feel thankful for this newfound ability you've developed. You're proud of yourself...

Some people claim that "happiness is a choice" and say that the secret to happiness is simply deciding that you want to be happy. This may not be true in the sense that we can change our mental state at will. But it is true in the sense that we can decide what we focus on, and we can decide *not* to have a bias that shuts out life's many blessings from our conscious awareness. We definitely have the choice not to go out of our way to interpret the world more negatively than it really is! **Happiness, then, is merely the choice to remove all those self-imposed filters and biases that keep us from enjoying what is already there**.

Rethink Toxic Relationships—Including the One You Have with Yourself

So much of every single day is automatic and unconscious. We resort to the same old patterns and habits without thinking about it or being aware that it's what we're doing. The negativity habit can be imprinted in our early formative years, sustained by our culture and society, and kept intact by our own set of narratives and core beliefs.

But people do not exist in a vacuum. No matter how personal and private your own thoughts, feelings, and core beliefs seem to you, they are in fact imbedded into the social environment around you. The relationships you have with others are constantly interacting with them, and there is mutual influence, for better or worse. All of this is to say that "negative thinking" can be like a house of cards—pull one card and you realize how many other cards fall as well because they were supported by it.

Your unique thought patterns and habits are in relationship with the unique thought patterns and habits of those around you. As you gain more awareness of the role that negativity plays in your life, you cannot help but notice how your relationships and general environment are all connected, too. To put it bluntly, if you have a problem with negativity, it's almost guaranteed that that negativity plays a role in your relationships with others.

A quick example will make this clear. Anne has worked really hard with a therapist to undo a whole complex web of negative core beliefs about herself. She can clearly see how her negative self-talk is jeopardizing her happiness, and how her distorted thought processes are making her miserable. She makes enormous strides and achieves genuine transformation, learning to defuse from difficult emotions and see herself—and the world—with completely different eyes. But somehow, it doesn't stick. She keeps finding herself back at square one and doesn't know why.

One day, her therapist gently suggests something: Could her husband be the reason? After gaining big insights into her behavior at every weekly therapy session, she then goes straight home and spends the remainder of the week with her husband, bickering. It's not that her husband is a bad person. Rather, it's that Anne has deeply entrenched patterns of negative behavior that *she plays out with him.*

Every day, there's a lot of complaining and fault finding, squabbles following some miscommunication, a little bit of sulking and stonewalling, a constant and low-grade level of irritation . . . all of it adding to a growing pile of resentment and negativity, every moment of every day. What chance did Anne's single therapy session have when pitched against all *that*?

The reason that Anne cannot make any improvements (or maintain the improvements she does make) is because she is not aware of the situations, relationships, and circumstances around her that are sustaining and creating her negativity. She is looking at the problem on one level (emotional, psychological, cognitive) and completely ignoring the other levels (social and relational). It's not that the work Anne is doing with her therapist is not useful—it's just that it doesn't go far enough. Importantly, it's not that Anne is a toxic person or that her husband is; rather, the relationship between them (i.e., their shared pattern of behavior) is toxic.

Once she realizes this, she goes back to her therapist, who encourages her to think strategically. What can she change, and what does she have to learn to cope with? How well is this pattern serving her life, and does she want to rewrite it?

To make the perspective shift that Anne has, you can ask yourself: what toxic behavioral patterns exist in your own life right now, and how do they interact with other people? **If relationships are shared patterns of behavior, what relationships in your life right now are part of a pattern of negativity?**

A Pattern Is Toxic; a Person Is Not

Before we go further, let's make a clear distinction: **There is no such thing as a "toxic person."** But the way a person relates to other people can certainly be toxic. After all, you may be reading this book because you have a pattern of negative thinking—but if you call yourself a "negative person," then you are saying that this pattern of behavior is fundamentally *who you are* . . . and that means that you cannot change. If you call yourself a person who has a pattern of negative thinking, then you are in control and can change. It's a big difference!

In the self-help realm, it has been trendy for a while now to go on "toxic person" witch hunts, i.e., identify anyone in your life who acts like a poison to you and forcefully remove them. While it may be one hundred percent true that another person treats you in abusive ways and negatively impacts your mental health and wellbeing, focusing exclusively on their role means you ignore your own. Thus, if Anne came to understand her husband as abusive, but called him "toxic" and simply left him . . . she might find herself in precisely the same kind of relationship once again. That's because she never understood and challenged her own patterns, so she promptly repeated them with someone else.

Remember that your unique thought patterns and habits *are in relationship* with the unique thought patterns and habits of those around you. If we think that the problem is merely that the other person is a jerk, we rob ourselves of a deeper understanding of our own ingrained relational patterns. For example, Anne might begin to understand that her negative thinking habit is actually part of a broader relational habit where she continually picks romantic partners who belittle and undermine her, because that fits with her core belief that she is worthless. If she merely blames her husband (who is, to be fair, to blame!), she never gives herself the chance to break that pattern within herself.

This is why it's so important to not lose sight of the fact that **relationships are shared patterns**. Anne's husband, should he find himself single again, may go back into the dating market and meet many new women . . . and none of them are interested in him because they are unwilling to tolerate his behavior. All alone in a room by himself, is he still "toxic"?

Anne might say, "He's an abuser; he makes me feel worthless," but this is not strictly true. It was Anne herself who first held the core belief that she was worthless. She then selected a partner who confirmed this and reflected it back to her. Again, neither Anne nor her husband are bad or toxic people. Rather, they both share in a mutual pattern of behavior that is toxic.

It's all too easy (and pretty tempting, if we're honest) to label people as toxic as though we didn't share equal responsibility for the quality of that relationship. But we do. And we commit to claiming our responsibility not because we want to take the "blame" but to better understand *why* our life is the way it is and what we can do to make it better.

What is a Toxic Relationship?

A toxic thought or feeling is one that has become so distorted and unhealthy that it is dramatically impairing your quality of life. A toxic relationship is the same. In CBT, you can challenge an unhelpful thought and rewrite it. But patterns are bigger than single thoughts, and they involve other people.

All relationships have some degree of difference, tension, and friction at times, but toxic relationships are more malignant; they

amplify and recreate negativity in a way that is destructive and unhealthy for all parties involved. You'll know that you're in a toxic relationship if one or both of you

- Feels devalued, disrespected, or abused
- Feels utterly exhausted, drained emotionally, and defeated
- Feels unsafe, either physically or emotionally
- Experience a constant state of drama, angst, and conflict
- Experience a loss of self-esteem and dignity
- Feels their boundaries are repeatedly violated
- Experiences chronic deceit, lies, or manipulation
- Experiences violence and aggression

Trying to undo negative thinking patterns when you're in a relationship like this is like trying to train for a marathon when you have cancer . . . i.e., not easy! Instead, you need to first remove yourself from relationships that are amplifying and sustaining negativity so that you can start to work on those patterns within yourself.

Here are a few tips to keep in mind as you broaden your perspective:

Tip 1: Turn your focus from the relationship to the relationship *dynamic*

Look beyond the current situation or disagreement and become curious about recurrent patterns. What keeps happening over and over again? What is the bigger picture? Sometimes, negative behaviors are just a once-off, but look to see if any repeating cycles can be found.

It's not about identifying the good guy and the bad guy, or deciding where to place blame, but rather asking, "What is actually happening here?" and being genuinely curious about the answer. Look at this broader pattern and ask yourself where it might have originally come from. Did you share this pattern with a caregiver as a child? Is this a coping mechanism you picked up after a particularly traumatic event in your past?

Tip 2: Be accountable

Ask what your role in the ongoing dynamic is, bearing in mind that this is not an exercise in shame or judgment. Rather, be honest about the ways that you've enabled the pattern to play out—or at least didn't stop it from playing out. It is vital to be able to call out bad behavior and identify abuse, but if we cling too tightly to the victim identity, we may forget our own power to change the situation.

What are your core beliefs about your role in life? How does that assumption manifest in your relationships right now? How are your thoughts and feelings sustaining the dynamic, and how are they challenging it?

Tip 3: Examine your core beliefs

Our relationships with others are a reflection of our relationship with ourselves, and vice versa. *Ask honestly what a current relationship is revealing about the core beliefs you have about yourself.* For example, if you find yourself repeatedly complaining that nobody takes you seriously, become curious about whether *you* hold a core belief that plays into this, and whether you don't take yourself seriously, either. The disrespectful people in your life are just one half of the story. The other half is the unconscious core belief you hold that you are not, in fact, worth anyone's respect.

If you change the core belief but keep the disrespectful people in your life, you have only solved half the problem. Likewise, if you get rid of the disrespectful people but maintain the core belief, then sooner or later, you will just attract new people much like the old people, who will continue to reflect that core belief back at you. To make real progress, you need to tackle both.

When You're the Toxic One . . .

The internet is awash with advice on how to deal with negative family members, partners, and friends, and long checklists to help you identify the narcissists, energy vampires, and toxic people you need to cut out of your life. But if you're the one who's toxic? Well . . . let's just say there aren't as many people interested in *that* material.

We'll now consider a delicate topic that can be difficult to talk about or even think about. The truth is that if we have a problem with negative thinking, we have the potential to be "toxic people" ourselves and bring the lion's share of negativity to our relationships. Again, being aware of these patterns is not about blame and shame. Rather, the more we are conscious of, the more we can be in control of.

Here is an exercise to help you identify the toxic and negative patterns you may be contributing to the relationships around you.

Step 1: Make a list

Sit down and compile a list of behaviors you know that you engage in habitually, positive or negative, major or minor. This takes some self-knowledge and honesty, but the exercises in the preceding chapters may have given you some useful insight. Don't list single behaviors or events, but ongoing and recurrent patterns. For example, you may list

Complaining about the weather

Going for "bad boys"

Making jokes in awkward situations

Gossiping and spreading rumors

Overworking

Minimizing achievements

Step 2: Understand the behavior

Look at the list and explore the results you're getting with each pattern of behavior. Look beyond whether the pattern feels good or how inevitable it seems, and consider instead whether it's working for you or not. Also ask where the behavior might have originally come from and what purpose it serves. The big thing to understand is what core beliefs may be at the root of this behavior.

For example, you may realize that your pattern of minimizing your own achievements is having a very negative effect on your life. You may know that it stems from growing up with very strict and critical parents who were sparing with praise. The core belief behind it all is, "You're nothing special." Now, not all your patterns of behavior are going to be big and serious—some will be fairly minor and insignificant.

Step 3: Put the pattern in context

This is the most important step. Ask yourself how this pattern of behavior fits into your bigger world. How is it sustained and maintained by the relationships around you? In what way might your own core beliefs be amplified by certain key relationships?

For example, you may look at your work life and realize that your bosses are happy to take advantage of the fact that you are a workaholic . . . without properly compensating you. Inadvertently, they are taking part in the "you're nothing special" dynamic and are an extension of it.

Step 4: Make changes both inside and out

Once you understand your own core beliefs and how they fit into bigger patterns of behavior with other people, you can start making changes. Do this on both levels:

1. Commit to making one small change to your inner thought processes, but also

2. take a step to changing your environment or relationship.

For example, you may start working on your self-esteem and start each morning with a mantra that counters the "I'm nothing special" core belief. At the same time, you can start putting up more boundaries at work and not agreeing to work overtime. You might also consider asking for a raise.

Of course, a pattern like overworking is a lot less noxious than the pattern of, say, gossiping and starting rumors. It can be far more difficult to be honest about these less-than-flattering habits we might have. Overeating, being lazy, avoiding responsibility, petty addictions, seeking revenge . . . these patterns are difficult to face, but they offer the biggest opportunity for growth if we're brave enough to face them.

Step 5: Be proud of yourself

It's important to stop and take stock of the changes you do make, even if they're small. Celebrate those wins—it's not easy making this kind of change. Give yourself credit where it's due and you'll find that the momentum will build, and next time, the process will be easier.

Summary

- We can understand the problem of negativity on different levels, from the physical to the psychological to the spiritual, evolutionary, or cultural. The psychological and emotional level is the easiest for us to change.
- The negativity bias is an evolved human tendency that conferred a survival advantage on our ancestors. It's the tendency to register and focus more readily on negative stimuli while ignoring or downplaying positive ones. If we are aware of it, we can take steps to mitigate its influence in personal relationships and decision-making.
- If you cannot rely on your brain to automatically and unconsciously look for the positive, then you will have to *deliberately* draw your attention to it instead. Use a gratitude journal and deliberately choose to focus on the positive.
- No man is an island. Your unique thought patterns and habits are in a constant relationship with the unique thought patterns and habits of those around you. Relationships are shared patterns, and there is no such thing as a toxic person, only toxic patterns, behaviors, and relationships.
- All relationships are occasionally difficult, but toxic relationships amplify and recreate negativity in a way that is destructive and unhealthy for all parties involved. Focus on

recurring dynamics and patterns rather than specific isolated behaviors, be accountable, and ask how your core beliefs are manifesting in the relationship.
- If you are bringing toxic patterns to a relationship, make a list of the behaviors, understand the function they are serving, put the pattern in context, then commit to making changes internally and externally.

Summary Guide

CHAPTER 1: REFRAME YOUR INTERNAL DIALOGUE AND TAKE CONTROL OF YOUR SELF-TALK

- How you think creates your life; negativity poisons everything in your world.
- Changing negativity requires a degree of metacognition (thinking about thinking) and a leap of faith to do something that hasn't been done before. Anyone can change their thought patterns; it requires only honest awareness and a willingness to take conscious and inspired action.
- Our mental shortcuts, assumptions, biases, and stereotypes are great at saving time and effort, but are not one hundred percent accurate one hundred percent of the time. The "all-or-nothing" disease is when we overextrapolate from one experience to other experiences we haven't had; we are making an error.
- Words have power, and our speech reflects our thought patterns. "Out of power" language is passive, self-victimizing, doubtful, angry, unconfident, fearful, excuse-making, or pessimistic, and can create a self-fulfilling prophesy.

- Become aware of your internal verbal habits. Then focus on what can be done, embrace nuance and shades of gray, and speak to yourself like you would a loved one.
- A cognitive distortion is a persistently incorrect belief, perception, or thought—for example, mental filtering, personalization, jumping to conclusions, mind-reading, catastrophizing, and using "should" statements and labels.
- Positive thinking is not just the absence of distortions, but thinking that helps you feel calm, hopeful, curious, grateful, stable, and confident.
- To challenge your inner critic, commit to not allowing your thoughts to dominate you. Gain psychological distance by labeling the thoughts as thoughts, not reality, and have self-compassion.
- Change happens outside your comfort zone, so realize that at some point, you'll need to take the leap and try something new.

CHAPTER 2: USE THE ABC METHOD AND WORK WITH A THOUGHT JOURNAL

- To rewrite our negative thought patterns, we "can't solve problems by using the same kind of thinking we used when we created them."
- We can use the ABCDE acronym (activating event, belief, consequence, disputation, and new event) and explore the stories we're telling in a thought journal. We can decide whether a new alternative is a good one according to its accuracy, helpfulness, and congruence with our values.
- Once you've identified your current thoughts, ask if there's a different way to think about things, and how you can bring that idea to life with concrete action. Seek out evidence for a new belief, practice self-compassion, and go into learning mode, asking questions instead of making statements.
- Negativity can be relieved by shifting perspectives and creating psychological distance. Remember that pessimism, negativity, and gloomy nihilism are all coping mechanisms and once served a purpose. But right now, we can choose to cope with adversity in different, healthier ways (and there always will be adversity!)
- Create spatial, temporal, and psychological distance from distressing thoughts, ask what others might do in our situation (role-switching), and turn your mind to concrete action instead of asking why. Focus on a small, concrete detail in the present and ask

what you can **do**. Avoid identifying problems without seeking solutions—i.e., complaining!
- When we are stuck in intense emotions, we can try the ACT technique of defusion. Imagine that your Mind is something separate from you and that you can watch it.
- Remember that you are not your thoughts; you are just having thoughts. Make your thoughts earn their keep!

CHAPTER 3: MASTER THE ART OF DISTRESS TOLERANCE

- We need distress tolerance skills to help us cope with extremely trying or painful moments, or emergency situations. When we're distressed, it's easy to slip back into old patterns of behavior or default to clumsy, destructive, or unconscious ways of coping—these are false coping mechanisms.
- Self-soothing is a way to acknowledge and accept pain that is inevitable—without making it any bigger than it should be. It is not distraction or avoidance, but about anchoring in the present using your five senses—a technique called grounding.

- TIPP stands for temperature, intense exercise, paced breathing, and paired muscle relaxation, all of which can help lower physiological arousal. Try cold water, vigorous movement, or breathing exercises to calm the limbic system.
- Practice radical acceptance, which doesn't mean we like what is happening, only that we have agreed to not fight with reality. Acknowledge how you feel and the reality of the situation and remind yourself of what matters.
- The ACCEPTS acronym (Activities, Contribute, Comparisons, Emotions, Push away, Thoughts, and Sensations) can help you better tolerate momentary distress—although not for the longer term.
- With anxiety, our goal is not to force ourselves not to worry, but to worry more efficiently. Scheduling worry time puts you in proactive control and helps you gain distance.
- Notice the anxiety, write down the time you'll postpone to—with the duration and content—then follow through as agreed.
- Mental noting and focused mundane tasks can help you turn anxious moments into opportunities for mindfulness.

CHAPTER 4: UPGRADE YOUR PSYCHOLOGICAL TOOLKIT WITH STOIC TECHNIQUES

- The ancient Stoics were masters of living in the present.
- One way of rethinking your relationship to the past is to adopt the Stoic attitude of *amor fati*. This translates roughly to "love of one's fate." Whatever happens is embraced, wanting "nothing to be different." To practice it, look at events as neutrally as possible and then respond to them with a simple mantra like "good." By focusing on action and solutions, we are able to transform adversity.
- Negative visualization is where we occasionally spend a short amount of time imagining in detail the negative things that could happen in life. This renews appreciation and gratitude for what matters, allows us to prepare for the future, and creates psychological resilience.
- With the "what-if" technique, we write down a fear and ask, "What if this were true?" and explore the worst that could happen, showing ourselves that it is tolerable and not

so bad after all. Likewise, remember *Memento mori*, Latin for, "remember that you will die" to help remind you of what matters.
- Problem-focused thinking zooms in on what's wrong. Solution-focused thinking zooms in on what *could* be right and looks to taking action to change the situation. Thinking needs to be balanced with action. Focus on the problem needs to be balanced with focus on the solution.
- Remember the Serenity Prayer and try the two-column exercise to help you identify what you can change and what you can't. Accept what you can't, act where you can. Ask what you want and value, then ask yourself, "Is what I'm doing, thinking, or feeling bringing me closer to that?"

CHAPTER 5: AVOID THE TRAP OF TOXIC POSITIVITY

- Toxic positivity is a kind of cognitive distortion and is an overgeneralization of a positive and optimistic attitude. It consists of denial, minimization, and invalidation of your own experience. Toxic positivity grows with shame, silence, and judgment. Positivity

itself isn't toxic, but denying our reality is. Human beings are wholes who contain both good and bad.
- We can embrace the *whole* instead of the *good* by watching the phrases we use, making friends with discomfort, being patient while we are in process, distinguishing between productive and unproductive negativity, and reconnecting to what we value and want to achieve in life. Ask yourself, "How does a person who values what I value behave when they experience what I'm experiencing?"
- Keeping a gratitude journal is a great way to create genuine feelings of positivity.
- Rather than creating good emotions and getting rid of negative ones, we can practice emotional self-regulation and become conscious masters of our own ever-unfolding emotional experience.
- What makes an emotion good or bad is the context and our own goals and values. We regulate when we decide which emotions to attend to, when, how, and for how long.
- Emotions have a life cycle, and we can manage those emotions at any point in the cycle—before the situation, during the situation, with our attention, with our cognitive appraisal, and finally, with our emotional response. Generally, the sooner

you intervene, the easier it is to modify the situation. Ask, "Is the way I'm thinking about this problem working for me right now?"

CHAPTER 6: WHERE DOES NEGATIVE THINKING REALLY COME FROM?

- We can understand the problem of negativity on different levels, from the physical to the psychological to the spiritual, evolutionary, or cultural. The psychological and emotional level is the easiest for us to change.
- The negativity bias is an evolved human tendency that conferred a survival advantage on our ancestors. It's the tendency to register and focus more readily on negative stimuli while ignoring or downplaying positive ones. If we are aware of it, we can take steps to mitigate its influence in personal relationships and decision-making.
- If you cannot rely on your brain to automatically and unconsciously look for the positive, then you will have to *deliberately* draw your attention to it instead. Use a gratitude journal and deliberately choose to focus on the positive.

- No man is an island. Your unique thought patterns and habits are in a constant relationship with the unique thought patterns and habits of those around you. Relationships are shared patterns, and there is no such thing as a toxic person, only toxic patterns, behaviors, and relationships.
- All relationships are occasionally difficult, but toxic relationships amplify and recreate negativity in a way that is destructive and unhealthy for all parties involved. Focus on recurring dynamics and patterns rather than specific isolated behaviors, be accountable, and ask how your core beliefs are manifesting in the relationship.
- If you are bringing toxic patterns to a relationship, make a list of the behaviors, understand the function they are serving, put the pattern in context, then commit to making changes internally and externally.

www.ingramcontent.com/pod-product-compliance
Lightning Source LLC
Chambersburg PA
CBHW020524080526
44583CB00013B/731